PLAY THROUGH THE BIBLE

A Toddler's Introduction to God's Word
Volume 1: Old Testament

Liz Millay

Steadfast Family
2018

Hear, O Israel: The LORD our God, the LORD is one. You shall love the LORD your God with all your heart and with all your soul and with all your might. And these words that I command you today shall be on your heart.

You shall teach them diligently to your children

and shall talk of them when you sit in your house, and when you walk by the way, and when you lie down, and when you rise. You shall bind them as a sign on your hand, and they shall be as frontlets between your eyes. You shall write them on the doorposts of your house and on your gates.

-Deuteronomy 6: 4-9 (NIV)

Safety note: The activities in this book are intended to be performed under adult supervision. Take caution with activities that call for materials such as scissors or small items that could be choking hazards. The recommendations in this book cannot replace common sense and judgement on proper safety procautions. The author does not hold any liability for mishap or injury that may occur from using the activities and ideas contained in this book.

Text, photography, and illustrations © 2018 by Liz Millay

First printing, 2018
www.steadfastfamily.com

to Kesed-
You're the reason this all started. I'm so glad you're my boy, and I'm proud of the young man you are becoming. Keep following God with all your heart. Mama loves you.

Contents

Introduction

When my oldest was two, I took to the internet looking for instruction and inspiration for how to begin teaching him the stories of the Bible. As I waded through Google searches and browsed Pinterest, I couldn't find quite what I was looking for. So, armed with our favorite storybook Bible and a shelf full of basic craft supplies, we paved our own way, playing through each story we read.

Four years later, the series of posts that shared our lessons is still the most popular content on my site. Perhaps you found it when you, like me, took to the internet with the question: "how do I teach my toddler the Bible?"

While the orginal series will always remain on the blog, I am so excited to be able to offer this updated and expanded book. After hearing from so many parents about how much their non-craft loving toddlers enjoyed and benefitted from the activity each week, I knew I wanted to expand the series to include all kinds of play.

Each child is unique and will learn in different ways. These lessons include a wide variety of activities so that you are able to chose what works for you and your child. Don't overwhelm yourself trying to do it all! Use this book as a guide and an inspiration. The orginal series was set up as weekly plans. You read one story a week and did a craft each day. For this book, there are no week or day numbers. Work through it from front to back or skip around at your choosing. It will work great either way!

In the same way, there is no set lesson format. You choose what Bible to read out of and when to do it. You choose what days and what activities and what order.

It is all flexible to work for you and your specific circumstance!

Finally, before you move on, I want to encourage you. Crafts and activities are a great way to help your child learn more and experience God's Word in a way that is fun and meaningful. However, it is not the be-all end-all of parental discipleship. The example you set and the love of God that flows from your own heart will make a greater impact than a craft ever could. Your continual prayers and caring instruction will grow your child's character in ways a game could never do. And in the end, though you are responsible for tending the garden of your child's soul, it is God who grows the fruit. My prayer is that this book is a help for you as you begin to disciple your child, but never a distraction or a burden.

I love to hear from those who have used Play Through the Bible! Use the hashtag #playthroughthebible on social media or send me a message through the Steadfast Family Facebook page or website. Seeing little ones loving to learn about God never ceases to warm my heart and fill me with gratitude.

Grace and peace,
Liz

> **Successful parenting is not about achieving goals (that you have no power to produce) but about being a usable and faithful tool in the hands of the One who alone is able to produce good things in your children.**
> **-Paul David Tripp**

Teaching the Bible to Toddlers

If you have ever tried to sit down the wild, loud, goofy being known as a toddler for "Bible time," then you know that standard teaching methods don't always apply! So, how do we reach these squirmy little ones to help them begin learning about having a relationship with God?

Here are some tips that will hopefully help!

#1 Think about long-term habits being built, not just the success of that particular day.
If your child can't remember you read a story about a man named Noah that morning - that's okay. They will remember with time. However, building the habit of going to God in His Word and through prayer and song and fun - that will be a habit that can be continued for the rest of your child's life.

#2 Don't view teaching the Bible as just a singular "event" during your day.
Toddlers are not made to sit down and focus on one thing for long periods of time, and learning about God is not supposed to be relegated to a twenty minute session in the day. Most of the ideas in this book are perfect for carrying throughout the day. Read the story of creation at breakfast and then talk about it as you go for a walk outside later. Read the story of Noah before naptime and then play out the story in the bath before bed. This fits perfectly with the command in Deuteronomy 6:7 to "talk about them when you sit at home and when you walk along the road, when you lie down and when you get up."

#3 If your child doesn't like to sit for a story, let them move!

Having them act out parts of the story is a great way to get them moving, while still listening to what you are reading. There are often ideas for this in the "teaching tips" section of the lessons. You can also read while they are playing nearby. You'll be surprised what they are hearing even if it doesn't seem like they are listening. Another great option is reading during a meal or snack time. They are stuck in a chair, with hands and mouths occupied! Makes for a great storytime.

#4 Remember the point of the activities.

If your child's craft ends up looking nothing like what it was supposed to or they want to play a game in a different way, that's totally okay! The point of all the activities is never a perfect finished product. The purpose is to use the activity as a way to keep talking about God's story. It's to be able to use the names of the Bible characters again. Most importantly, it is a way to speak truths to little ears about who God is.

#5 Keep it simple.

While I definitely wouldn't be afraid to talk with your child about things that are over their head (they pick up on so much!), I also recommend keeping your goals simple. Learn the names of the characters. Learn the basic parts of the story. Don't worry about tying everything up with a neat moral or learning lesson. Just let this be a time of introduction to God's amazing story. As your child grows you will continue to return to these stories, learning their truths more in depth every time.

And above all else remember, if your Bible teaching time plans don't go exactly how you planned, don't get discouraged! Keep being faithful and let God work to reach your child's heart.

Choosing a Storybook Bible

If you've ever walked into a Christian bookstore or searched Amazon, then you know that the number of storybook Bible options out there is crazy overwhelming! Where do you even start when it comes to choosing one for your child?

It is helpful to have a set of criteria when making your selection. Critera that leads to a happy toddler *and* a happy adult reader, not to mention leads to the start of building a love for God's Word!

Here are my top three criteria for choosing a storybook Bible:

#1 Biblical Accuracy
When it comes to storybook Bibles, this is the number one concern. In our attempts to make the stories digestible to children, are we staying true to the meaning of the actual Biblical text? Does the author go a little too deep into their imagination, weaving a story that may not actually be implied in the original text?

On the flip-side, are the most important elements are included? This can especially happen with children's Bibles that like to gloss over the more uncomfortable aspects of the Bible. While no children's Bible is going to cover all the dark, nitty gritty moments in the Bible (nor should they), look for one that covers the most important aspects.

Finally, are the stories dumbed down? You'll find this especially in the story Bibles that are marketed towards the very youngest listeners. While you definitely want stories that are simple, you also want to give plenty of information that can be discussed, dwelt on, and grown into. Little ones often understand and absorb more than we give them credit for!

#2 Lovely Illustrations
Beautiful illustrations may not seem like *that* big of a deal, but I can assure you, once you've glanced through some of the downright goofy looking children's Bible cartoons, lovely pictures are a nice change of pace. Plus, for many young children it is the images in the Bible that will capture their attention and imagination moreso than the actual text. Give them something lovely to look at and dwell on.

#3 Engaging Text
Besides being Biblically accurate, an engaging story is probably the most important part of any children's Bible. If your child isn't interested in listening to the stories, reading them isn't going to do a whole lot. Children aren't usually interested in flowery language, nor do they want to sit through something dry and monotone. Look for something that communicates the story well, while also staying simple.

I highly recommend owning multiple different storybook Bibles and switching between them. Not every story is included in each bible either, so having more than one will give you a greater selection as well. The library can often be a great place to "test run" different versions. If you need more help making your selection, check out our top recommendations in the appendix!

One final note: don't be afraid to read to your toddler from the actual Bible. It is never too early to begin introducing them to the wonder of God's Word. Looking up the memory verses in a "special Bible" is a great place to start!

The Parts of the Lessons

Before you get started, take a moment to familiarize yourself with the parts of the lessons.

On the first page of each Bible story, you will find the introductory material.

First is the story and the reference where it can be found.

Then there is a memory verse. If your child is too young to memorize the whole verse, that's okay! You can shorten it down, or just take time to look it up and read it together from a "big Bible." Even if they don't quite understand the words, they will start to see the importance of God's special words in the Bible.

In the blue circle is the focus points for the story. For every story except Creation, there are two focus points: one is about the characters in the story and one is about what God is doing in the story. Sometimes, there is a lot going on in these stories - the focus point helps give you direction on what to hone in on with your child.

Next is the guided discussion. Something I noticed early on when discussing Bible stories with my toddler is that they liked to have the same conversations over and over. These conversations often had a catechism-like feel with me asking questions and him giving short replies. He loved the feeling of knowing the answers! The guided discussion included with each story is a starting point for your dicussions with your toddler.

The final section on this page is the teaching tips. These are a variety of helpful hints to use while teaching your toddler each story.

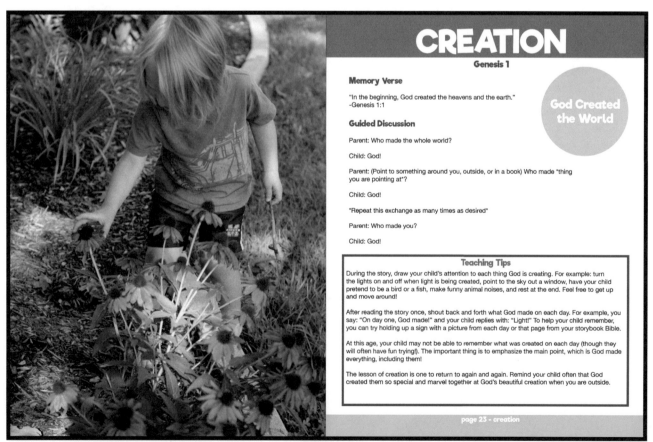

CREATION
Genesis 1

Memory Verse

"In the beginning, God created the heavens and the earth."
-Genesis 1:1

Guided Discussion

Parent: Who made the whole world?

Child: God!

Parent: (Point to something around you, outside, or in a book) Who made *thing you are pointing at*?

Child: God!

Repeat this exchange as many times as desired

Parent: Who made you?

Child: God!

God Created the World

Teaching Tips

During the story, draw your child's attention to each thing God is creating. For example: turn the lights on and off when light is being created, point to the sky out a window, have your child pretend to be a bird or a fish, make funny animal noises, and rest at the end. Feel free to get up and move around!

After reading the story once, shout back and forth what God made on each day. For example, you say: "On day one, God made!" and your child replies with: "Light!" To help your child remember, you can try holding up a sign with a picture from each day or that page from your storybook Bible.

At this age, your child may not be able to remember what was created on each day (though they will often have fun trying!). The important thing is to emphasize the main point, which is God made everything, including them!

The lesson of creation is one to return to again and again. Remind your child often that God created them so special and marvel together at God's beautiful creation when you are outside.

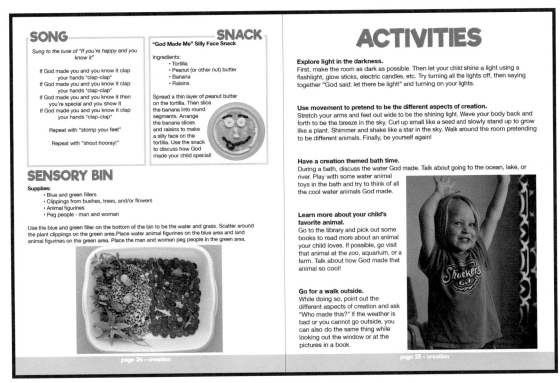

Image content (page 24-25 of creation booklet):

SONG

Sung to the tune of "If you're happy and you know it"

If God made you and you know it clap
your hands "clap-clap"
If God made you and you know it clap
your hands "clap-clap"
If God made you and you know it then
you're special and you show it
If God made you and you know it clap
your hands "clap-clap"

Repeat with "stomp your feet"

Repeat with "shout hooray!"

SNACK

"God Made Me" Silly Face Snack

Ingredients:
• Tortilla
• Peanut (or other nut) butter
• Banana
• Raisins

Spread a thin layer of peanut butter on the tortilla. Then slice the banana into round segments. Arrange the banana slices and raisins to make a silly face on the tortilla. Use the snack to discuss how God made your child special!

SENSORY BIN

Supplies:
• Blue and green fillers
• Clippings from bushes, trees, and/or flowers
• Animal figurines
• Peg people - man and woman

Use the blue and green filler on the bottom of the bin to be the water and grass. Scatter around the plant clippings on the green area. Place water animal figurines on the blue area and land animal figurines on the green area. Place the man and woman peg people in the green area.

ACTIVITIES

Explore light in the darkness.
First, make the room as dark as possible. Then let your child shine a light using a flashlight, glow sticks, electric candles, etc. Try turning all the lights off, then saying together "God said: let there be light!" and turning on your lights.

Use movement to pretend to be the different aspects of creation.
Stretch your arms and feet out wide to be the shining light. Wave your body back and forth to be the breeze in the sky. Curl up small like a seed and slowly stand up to grow like a plant. Shimmer and shake like a star in the sky. Walk around the room pretending to be different animals. Finally, be yourself again!

Have a creation themed bath time.
During a bath, discuss the water God made. Talk about going to the ocean, lake, or river. Play with some water animal toys in the bath and try to think of all the cool water animals God made.

Learn more about your child's favorite animal.
Go to the library and pick out some books to read more about an animal your child loves. If possible, go visit that animal at the zoo, aquarium, or a farm. Talk about how God made that animal so cool!

Go for a walk outside.
While doing so, point out the different aspects of creation and ask "Who made this?" If the weather is bad or you cannot go outside, you can also do the same thing while looking out the window or at the pictures in a book.

page 24 - creation   page 25 - creation

Next you will find three ideas that go along with the theme of the story. The first is either a classic kid's Bible song or a new song set to a familiar tune. The second is a snack idea. This is not meant to be food art! All of the ideas are quick and simple, made with basic food items that kids generally enjoy. Finally, there is a sensory bin - a simple way for your child to play out the story. On the next page are five ideas for additional activities you can do to reinforce the story. You'll find pretend play ideas, games, and more! Some of my personal favorites are the things you can do as part of your daily life. They are great ways to keep talking about God with your child throughout the day!

On the final spread you will find the crafts to go along with the story. There are five, so pick and choose the ones you want to do or do one every day. It's up to you! Just remember that the goal of the crafts is not a pretty end product. It's to be able to continue the conversations about the story you are learning in a fun way.

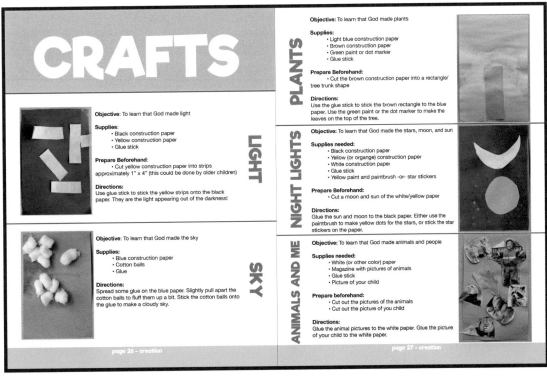

Image content (page 26-27 of creation booklet):

CRAFTS

LIGHT

Objective: To learn that God made light

Supplies:
• Black construction paper
• Yellow construction paper
• Glue stick

Prepare Beforehand:
• Cut yellow construction paper into strips approximately 1" x 4" (this could be done by older children)

Directions:
Use glue stick to stick the yellow strips onto the black paper. They are the light appearing out of the darkness!

SKY

Objective: To learn that God made the sky

Supplies:
• Blue construction paper
• Cotton balls
• Glue

Directions:
Spread some glue on the blue paper. Slightly pull apart the cotton balls to fluff them up a bit. Stick the cotton balls onto the glue to make a cloudy sky.

PLANTS

Objective: To learn that God made plants

Supplies:
• Light blue construction paper
• Brown construction paper
• Green paint or dot marker
• Glue stick

Prepare Beforehand:
• Cut the brown construction paper into a rectangle/tree trunk shape

Directions:
Use the glue stick to stick the brown rectangle to the blue paper. Use the green paint or the dot marker to make the leaves on the top of the tree.

NIGHT LIGHTS

Objective: To learn that God made the stars, moon, and sun

Supplies needed:
• Black construction paper
• Yellow (or organge) construction paper
• White construction paper
• Glue stick
• Yellow paint and paintbrush -or- star stickers

Prepare Beforehand:
• Cut a moon and sun of the white/yellow paper

Directions:
Glue the sun and moon to the black paper. Either use the paintbrush to make yellow dots for the stars, or stick the star stickers on the paper.

ANIMALS AND ME

Objective: To learn that God made animals and people

Supplies needed:
• White (or other color) paper
• Magazine with pictures of animals
• Glue stick
• Picture of your child

Prepare beforehand:
• Cut out the pictures of the animals
• Cut out the picture of you child

Directions:
Glue the animal pictures to the white paper. Glue the picture of your child to the white paper.

page 26 - creation   page 27 - creation

Supplies and Supply Storage

One thing that was very important to me as I created this book was to keep the required supplies very simple. Besides a few items, most of the supplies are things you likely already have on hand or are super easy to grab from the store.

For the crafts, the most common supplies that you will want to always have on hand are:

- A variety of colors of construction paper
- Glue sticks
- Liquid glue
- Crayons and/or markers
- Dot markers and/or paint and brushes
- Paper plates
- Recycling materials

You will also need some supplies for the sensory bins, but again most are common household items. For the majority of bins you will need some kind of filler material: rice, beans, stones, etc. Beans, pasta, and rice can all be dyed with food coloring to get a specific color. For the bin itself, you can use a storage bin, water table, or any kind of container you happen to have on hand. The bin shown in the pictures throughout the book is a dish tub from the dollar store.

And please note, if you don't have something, feel free to substitute. My children have been known to play pretend people with their silverware, so most substitutions will be no problem for your child's imagination!

To make it super easy for yourself when you get ready to do your crafts or activities, I recommend gathering all your materials together beforehand so they are ready to go. Store your supplies in a special cabinet or on a shelf. Rolling carts are also a super convienient way to keep your materials organized.

Craft Storage

Even if your child only completed half of the crafts in this book, that is still a LOT of crafts laying around. To prevent yourself from being buried under a mountation of glue and construction paper, here are two ideas to help qwell the clutter and make it so your child can continue to interact with and enjoy his or her artwork.

Idea #1 - Wire Pinned Gallery

Hang a long string of wire across an open wall space and use clothespins to attach artwork for display. This is perfect for those "extra speicial" pieces.

Idea #2 - Artwork Binder

Most of the crafts in this book are able to be three hole punched and placed in a binder. This creates a book of your child's artwork, perfect for paging through and reminiscing on the stories you've learned!

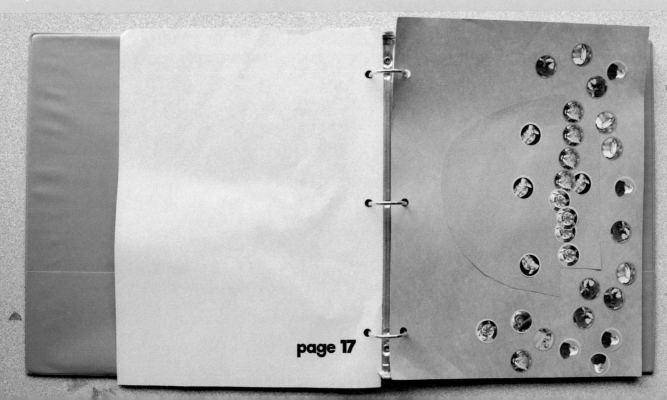

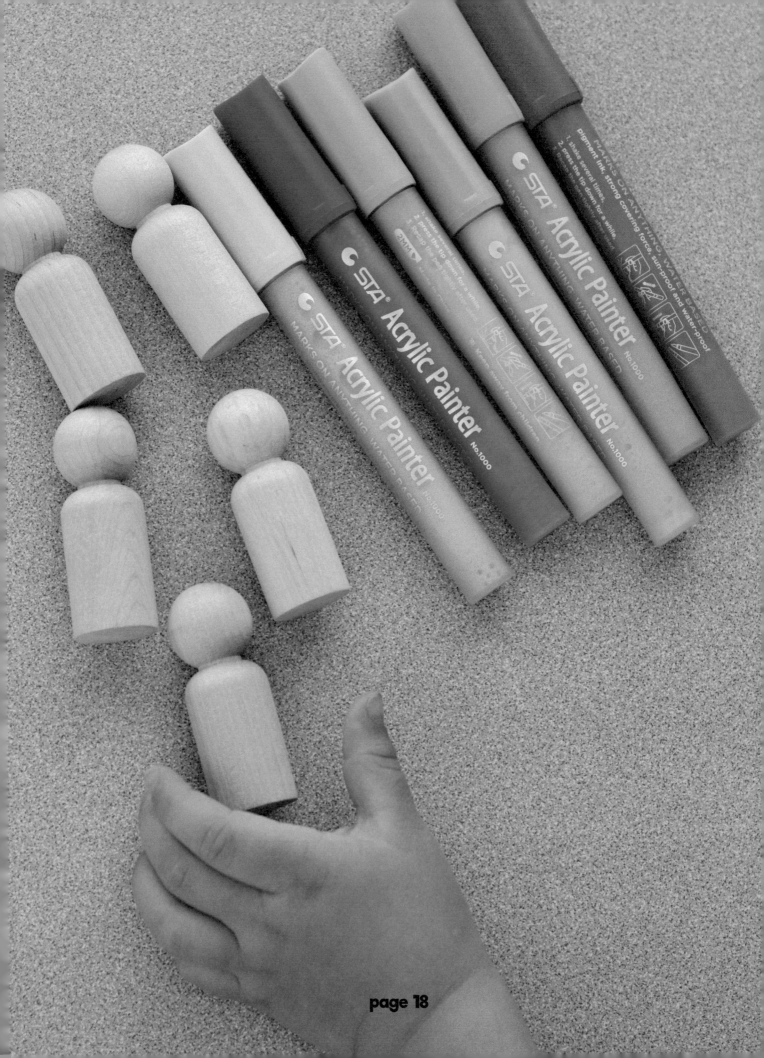

Peg People

Wooden peg people are used in most of the lessons as an element in the sensory bin. However, even if you don't use them in a sensory bin, they are still great for pretend play acting out the stories. Yes, you can definitely use any toy people figurines you have on hand, but these are great fun to make and play with! Worried you aren't artistic enough to paint them? No problem! Just hand the supplies over to your toddler, I guarentee they won't feel the same hesistation!

Supplies needed:
- Unfinished wooden peg dolls
- Acrylic paint pens
- Sealer such as Mod-Podge (optional)

Process:

Use the paint pens to add clothes, hair, and faces to the unfinished peg dolls. You can also use regular acrylic paints, but I found the paint pens to be far easier and less messy! You can even use sharpies or washable markers, although the color won't be as vibrant!

You can make specific Bible characters or leave them more vague to use for multiple stories. Be sure to make men and women, young and old! We even added just the face to two of the peg dolls to be Adam and Eve!

Most of all, have fun with it! You may just find the process addictive and end up with a whole slew of peg people for playing Bible stories!

Lessons and Activities

CREATION

Genesis 1

Memory Verse

"In the beginning, God created the heavens and the earth."
-Genesis 1:1

God Created
the World

Guided Discussion

Parent: Who made the whole world?

Child: God!

Parent: (Point to something around you, outside, or in a book) Who made *thing you are pointing at*?

Child: God!

Repeat this exchange as many times as desired

Parent: Who made you?

Child: God!

Teaching Tips

During the story, draw your child's attention to each thing God is creating. For example: turn the lights on and off when light is being created, point to the sky out a window, have your child pretend to be a bird or a fish, make funny animal noises, and rest at the end. Feel free to get up and move around!

After reading the story once, shout back and forth what God made on each day. For example, you say: "On day one, God made!" and your child replies with: "Light!" To help your child remember, you can try holding up a sign with a picture from each day or that page from your storybook Bible.

At this age, your child may not be able to remember what was created on each day (though they will often have fun trying!). The important thing is to emphasize the main point, which is God made everything, including them!

The lesson of creation is one to return to again and again. Remind your child often that God created them so special and marvel together at God's beautiful creation when you are outside.

SONG

Sung to the tune of "If you're happy and you know it"

If God made you and you know it clap
your hands *clap-clap*
If God made you and you know it clap
your hands *clap-clap*
If God made you and you know it then
you're special and you show it
If God made you and you know it clap
your hands *clap-clap*

Repeat with "stomp your feet"

Repeat with "shout hooray!"

SNACK

"God Made Me" Silly Face Snack

Ingredients:
- Tortilla
- Peanut (or other nut) butter
- Banana
- Raisins

Spread a thin layer of peanut butter on the tortilla. Then slice the banana into round segments. Arrange the banana slices and raisins to make a silly face on the tortilla. Use the snack to discuss how God made your child special!

SENSORY BIN

Supplies:
- Blue and green fillers
- Clippings from bushes, trees, and/or flowers
- Animal figurines
- Peg people - man and woman

Use the blue and green filler on the bottom of the bin to be the water and grass. Scatter around the plant clippings on the green area. Place water animal figurines on the blue area and land animal figurines on the green area. Place the man and woman peg people in the green area.

ACTIVITIES

Explore light in the darkness.
First, make the room as dark as possible. Then let your child shine a light using a flashlight, glow sticks, electric candles, etc. Try turning all the lights off, then saying together "God said: let there be light!" and turning on your lights.

Use movement to pretend to be the different aspects of creation.
Stretch your arms and feet out wide to be the shining light. Wave your body back and forth to be the breeze in the sky. Curl up small like a seed and slowly stand up to grow like a plant. Shimmer and shake like a star in the sky. Walk around the room pretending to be different animals. Finally, be yourself again!

Have a creation themed bath time.
During a bath, discuss the water God made. Talk about going to the ocean, lake, or river. Play with some water animal toys in the bath and try to think of all the cool water animals God made.

Learn more about your child's favorite animal.
Go to the library and pick out some books to read more about an animal your child loves. If possible, go visit that animal at the zoo, aquarium, or a farm. Talk about how God made that animal so amazing!

Go for a walk outside.
While doing so, point out the different aspects of creation and ask "Who made this?" If the weather is bad or you cannot go outside, you can also do the same thing while looking out the window or at the pictures in a book.

CRAFTS

Objective: To learn that God made light

Supplies:
- Black construction paper
- Yellow construction paper
- Glue stick

Prepare Beforehand:
- Cut yellow construction paper into strips approximately 1" x 4"

Directions:
Use glue stick to stick the yellow strips onto the black paper. They are the light appearing out of the darkness!

Objective: To learn that God made the sky

Supplies:
- Blue construction paper
- Cotton balls
- Glue

Directions:
Spread some glue on the blue paper. Slightly pull apart the cotton balls to fluff them up a bit. Stick the cotton balls onto the glue to make a cloudy sky.

Objective: To learn that God made plants

Supplies:
- Light blue construction paper
- Brown construction paper
- Green paint or dot marker
- Glue stick

Prepare Beforehand:
- Cut the brown construction paper into a rectangle/ tree trunk shape

Directions:
Use the glue stick to stick the brown rectangle to the blue paper. Use the green paint or the dot marker to make the leaves on the top of the tree.

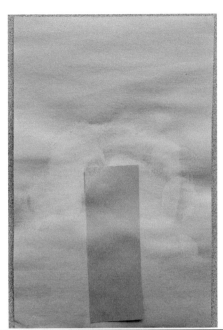

Objective: To learn that God made the stars, moon, and sun

Supplies needed:
- Black construction paper
- Yellow (or organge) construction paper
- White construction paper
- Glue stick
- Yellow paint/paintbrush or star stickers

Prepare Beforehand:
- Cut a moon and sun of the white/yellow paper

Directions:
Glue the sun and moon to the black paper. Either use the paintbrush to make yellow dots for the stars, or stick the star stickers on the paper.

Objective: To learn that God made animals and people

Supplies needed:
- White (or other color) paper
- Magazine with pictures of animals
- Glue stick
- Picture of your child

Prepare beforehand:
- Cut out the pictures of the animals
- Cut out the picture of you child

Directions:
Glue the animal pictures to the paper. Glue the picture of your child to the paper.

ADAM + EVE

Genesis 2-3

Memory Verse

"Therefore, just as sin came into the world through one man, and death through sin, and so death spread to all men because all sinned" Romans 5:12 (ESV)

Guided Discussion

Parent: What did God tell Adam and Eve?

Child: Don't eat from the tree!

Parent: Did they obey God?

Child: No.

Parent: No, they didn't. Could they stay with God now?

Child: No.

Parent: No, they couldn't. It was very sad because God loved them so much.

Adam and Eve Disobeyed God
- - -
God Loved Adam and Eve

Teaching Tips

Focus on the simple task of remembering the names of the people in the stories. Learning the names of the characters is an important part of your child's foundation in the Bible. Next time you go over the story, when they are a little older and ready to learn and understand a little more, they will remember those characters like old friends.

When reading the story of Adam and Eve, pause frequently to review what God said: "Don't eat the fruit." For example, when Eve is considering eating the fruit, ask your child "Did God say they could eat the fruit?" Pretty much every toddler in the world will enjoy saying "No!"

When you get to the end of the story, emphasize what is going on by reading it in a sad voice. Sad that Adam and Eve didn't obey God. Sad that they did something bad. Sad that the world has bad things in it now. Sad that they can't live with God anymore.

This is a good time to skip right to the end of the story and have a gospel conversation! Don't leave it at "sin entered the world," let your child know about the One who came to save us from our sin. God promised Adam and Eve that someone would come and crush sin - that person is Jesus!

SONG

Sung to the tune of "Down by the Bay"

Down in the garden
Where the fruit tree grows
Not supposed to eat it
Oh everybody knows!
For when they do
Then God will say
You listened to the snake, you made a mistake
You didn't obey

Down in the garden
Where the fruit tree grows
Not supposed to eat it
Oh everybody knows!
For when they do
Then God will say
I still love you, and I'll save you soon
But you didn't obey

SNACK

"Good Fruit" Snack

Ingredients:
• Variety of fruit

Wash, peel, and slice fruit as necessary. Arrange fruit on the plate. Discuss how God told Adam and Eve to *not* eat a certain fruit. What kind of fruit do they think it was? Talk more about the story together.

SENSORY BIN

Supplies:
• Green filler
• Clippings from bushes, trees, and/or flowers
• Snake figurine
• Peg people - man and woman
• Small circles cut out of paper

Place the green filler in the bottom of the bin to be the grass. Place in the clippings to create a garden environment. Place the circles in one of the plant clippings to be the tree with the fruit. Set in the snake and the two peg people.

ACTIVITIES

Spend some time in a garden.
Whether you have a big garden you can care for, or you just plant a few seeds in a small pot, spend some time caring for plants. If you don't have a garden of your own, try visiting a local community garden or bontanical garden. Use this time to talk about how Adam and Eve lived in the garden God made and had to care for the plants and animals there.

Play the animal name game.
Gather together some animal toys. Tell your child that one of Adam's jobs in the garden was to name the animals. Spend some time playing with the animals and letting your child come up with names for all of them.

Build a tree out of blocks.
Using blocks like Duplos or Megabloks, build a tree with fruit on it. Use the time playing with blocks to talk about Adam and Eve disobeying God and eating the fruit from the tree.

"Don't eat the fruit" game.
Place some balls on a chair to be the fruit in the tree. Have your child stand between you and the fruit. You try and sneak over to take some of the fruit, but have them say "God said don't eat the fruit!" If they tag you, you have to go back to where you started and try again.

Use the garden scene you created.
Take the puppets, tree, and snake and set them into front of the garden scene. Use them to act out the story and play pretend.

CRAFTS

Objective: To learn who Adam is

Supplies:
- Any color construction paper
- Tan construction paper
- Glue stick
- Craft stick
- Markers or crayons

Prepare Beforehand:
- Cut the tan paper into a circle for the head, and four long and skinny rectangles for the arms and feet
- Cut a long rectangle out of the other color paper

Directions:
Glue the cut out pieces of paper into the shape of a man. Glue the man onto the craft stick to make a puppet. Use the markers or crayons to add a face and decorate as desired.

ADAM

Objective: To learn who Eve is

Supplies:
- Any color construction paper
- Tan construction paper
- Glue stick
- Craft stick
- Markers or crayons

Prepare Beforehand:
- Cut the tan paper into a circle for the head, and four long and skinny rectangles for the arms and feet
- Cut a long triangle out of the other color paper

Directions:
Same as above.

EVE

Objective: To learn that God told Adam and Eve not to eat from the tree

Supplies:
- Toilet paper roll tube
- Green construction paper
- Red dot marker or red paint and paintbrush

Prepare Beforehand:
- Cut a tree-top shape out of the green paper
- Cut two slits in the top of the toilet paper roll tube

Directions:
Use the dot marker or paint to make fruit on the tree-top. Slide the green tree-top into the slits on the toilet paper roll tube.

Objective: To learn that a snake tricked Eve

Supplies needed:
- White paper plate
- Markers or crayons
- Googly eyes (optional)

Prepare Beforehand:
- Trace the outline of a snake on the paper plate in a spiral and then cut it out

Directions:
Use the crayons or markers to decorate the snake. Place the googly eyes on the snake's head.

Objective: To learn that Adam and Eve lived in the garden

Supplies needed:
- Two pieces of paper (blue or white)
- Markers or crayons
- Glue or tape

Prepare beforehand:
- Fold up one of the long sides of a paper (this will be the bottom of the back). Draw a simple garden on the front

Directions:
Color in the garden scene. Take the second piece of blue paper and fold it in half, then fold in each side about an inch. Glue the flaps you just created to the back of your garden scene to create curve that will hold your scene up.

NOAH
Genesis 6-8

Memory Verse

"Noah did everything just as God commanded him."
-Genesis 6:22 (NIV)

Guided Discussion

Parent: Did Noah obey God?

Child: Yes.

Parent: Were the other people obeying God?

Child: No.

Parent: No, that's right. They were being mean and bad. How did that make God feel?

Child: Sad.

Parent: What happened when Noah obeyed God?

Child: God kept him safe!

Teaching Tips

In the story of Noah, we often focus on how Noah obeyed God. This is a really important point! Noah was the only one on earth who found favor in God's eyes. However, it is also important to make a second point - God saved Noah. While at this age a focus on learning about the people in the Bible stories is good and normal, don't completely forget who the real hero of these stories is - God!

While reading, use fun motions like: stretching your arms out wide for the big boat, pretend to hammer the boat, wiggle your fingers for the rain, make animal noises, etc.

When you are finished reading the story, talk about how God was sad because no one was obeying him and everyone was being mean and bad. Make sad faces. Then talk about how Noah obeyed God. Smile and make a thumbs up or clap for Noah.

Flip back in your storybook Bible to the story of Adam and Eve. Ask: "Did Adam and Eve obey God?"

SONG

Sung to the tune of "Row Row Row Your Boat"

Build, build, build a boat
Make it big and strong
Joyfully, joyfully, joyfully, joyfully
Obey God all day long

Fill, fill, fill the boat
Bring the animals on
Joyfully, joyfully, joyfully, joyfully
Obey God all day long

Ride, ride, ride the boat
It's raining hard and long
Joyfully, joyfully, joyfully, joyfully
Obey God all day long

Off, off, off the boat
You're safe now sing a song
Joyfully, joyfully, joyfully, joyfully
Obey God all day long

SNACK

Animals in the Ark

Ingredients:
- Animal crackers
- Peanut (or other nut) butter
- Banana

Spread peanut butter on the inside curve of the banana. Place the animal crackers in the peanut butter on the banana "boat." Talk about how God kept Noah and the animals safe inside the boat.

SENSORY BIN

Supplies:
- Water
- Waterproof container
- Animal figurines
- Plastic people figurines
- Blue food coloring (optional)
- Blue gems (optional)

Fill the bin up a third to a half of the way with water. Add a few drops of blue food coloring (optional). Add the gems and water animals to the water, if using. Place in the waterproof container and fill with animals and people.

ACTIVITIES

Build boats like Noah.
Use blocks (or another type of construction toy) to build a boat. Add people and animal figurines if desired.

Be Noah in the boat.
Gather up some stuffed animals and a laundry basket. Tell your child he or she gets to pretend to be Noah and put all the animals in the laundry basket "boat." Then, he or she can climb in and sail the boat through the storm. Put a blue blanket under the "boat" and shake it for the "waves." Finally, take all the animals out when the storm has passed and the flood is over.

Play animal pretend.
Pretend to be the different animals that went in the ark with Noah. Stomp like elephants, bark like dogs, stretch like cats, fly like birds, slither like snakes, etc. If you'd like, turn on some music while you pretend to be the animal. When you turn the music off freeze! Then do it again with another animal.

Go bird watching.
Either go outside or look out the window to see what birds you can find. While you are waiting and looking, talk about how Noah waited for a dove to know if the flood was gone.

Go on a rainbow scavenger hunt.
Talk about how God sent a rainbow after the flood. Then, work together to try and find something in the room that is each of the colors of the rainbow.

CRAFTS

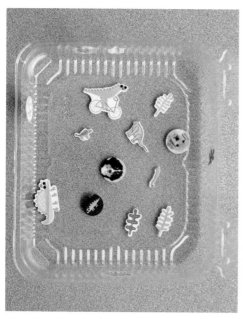

Objective: To learn that Noah obeyed God and built an ark

Supplies:
- Waterproof plastic container (such as a recycled salad container)
- Stickers (including animals, if possible)

Directions:
Use the stickers to decorate the plastic container "boat." If you have animal stickers, stick them onto the inside of the boat. If desired, use this boat for the sensory bin play.

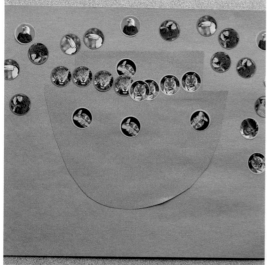

Objective: To learn that animals came in the ark with Noah

Supplies:
- Brown construction paper
- Blue construction paper
- Animal stickers
- Glue stick

Prepare Beforehand:
- Cut ark shapes out of the brown paper - a half circle for the bottom and a rectangle for the top

Directions:
Glue the ark shapes onto the blue paper. Stick the animal stickers on and around the ark.

FLOATING BOAT

Objective: To learn that everyone in the ark was safe

Supplies:
- Blue, brown, and white construction paper
- Craft stick
- Glue stick
- Blue and gray markers or crayons

Prepare Beforehand:
- Cut a long strip of waves out of blue paper
- Cut a small ark shape out of the brown paper

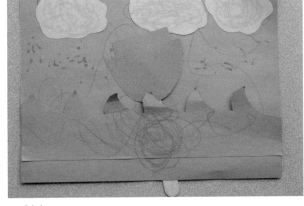

Directions:
Make a cut a third of the way from the bottom of a piece of blue paper. Glue the waves just below the line you cut out. Color the white clouds with the gray marker and glue in the sky. Use the blue marker to add rain. Glue the brown ark to a craft stick to make a small puppet. Slide the puppet through the slit on the paper to make it "float" in the water.

THE DOVE

Objective: To learn that Noah sent out a dove to see if the land had appeared again

Supplies:
- White paper plate
- Googly eyes
- Orange or yellow construction paper
- White feathers
- Glue

Directions:
Fold the paper plate in half. Glue the feathers on to make the wings and the tail. Place the googly eyes on either side of one corner. Cut a triangle out of the orange or yellow paper and glue on to make the beak.

RAINBOW PROMISE

Objective: To learn that God sent a rainbow to promise he would never flood the earth again

Supplies:
- White paper
- Construction paper in rainbow colors
- Glue stick

Prepare Beforehand:
- Cut small squares out of all the colors of paper.
- Make rainbow shaped guide lines on the white paper where the squares will be glued down

Directions:
Glue the different color paper squares to the white paper in the shape of a rainbow.

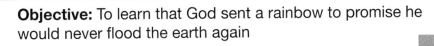

ABRAHAM + SARAH

Genesis 12-21

Memory Verse

"Now the Lord was gracious to Sarah as he had said, and the Lord did for Sarah what he had promised." -Genesis 21:1 (NIV)

Abraham Had Faith - - - God Kept His Promise

Guided Discussion

Parent: What did Abraham and Sarah want most of all?

Child: A baby boy.

Parent: Did they think they would ever have one?

Child: No.

Parent: Did God say they'd have a baby?

Child: Yes.

Parent: Did God keep his promise?

Child: Yes!

Parent: Yes, he did. God always keeps his promises.

Teaching Tips

Abraham is a fun name to say, but it can be a little tricky. Good thing little kids often love saying big words! Take a moment to practice saying it a few times.

Ask your child what they want more than anything in the whole world. Talk about how the one thing that Abraham and Sarah wanted was to have a baby boy.

One of the best parts of this story is the illustration that Abraham would have as many descendants as stars in the sky. However, metaphors like this can be confusing for literal thinking toddlers. That's okay! Just focus on the basics of the story, letting them grasp what is within their reach. Their understanding will continue to develop as they grow and mature.

When you get to the part of the story where God tells Abraham to go on a long journey, go on your own pretend journey. You can do it right there in your seats or get up and go for a walk around your house.

SONG

Father Abraham

Father Abraham had many sons
Many sons had Father Abraham
I am one of them and so are you
So let's all praise the Lord
Right arm!

Father Abraham had many sons
Many sons had Father Abraham
I am one of them and so are you
So let's all praise the Lord
Right arm, left arm!

Father Abraham had many sons
Many sons had Father Abraham
I am one of them and so are you
So let's all praise the Lord
Right arm, left arm, right foot!
...continuing on...

SNACK

Abraham's Starry Snack

Ingredients:
- Sliced cheese
- Circle crackers
- Small star cookie cutter

Use the cookie cutter to cut stars out of the cheese. Place each star on a cracker. Talk about God's promise to Abraham.

SENSORY BIN

Supplies:
- Brown construction paper
- Two peg people - woman and man
- Sand (or other filler)
- Animal figurines (camels, donkeys, sheep, etc) - optional

Fill the bottom of the bin with sand (or an alternate filler). Fold the brown construction paper into a tent shape. Place in the peg people and animals, if using. Pretend play Abraham's journey!

ACTIVITIES

Make a fort.
Using sheets or blankets, make a tent like the one Abraham and Sarah lived in. Have fun pretending to be Abraham and Sarah! If desired, use a baby doll to be Isaac. This is a great activity for practicing the names in the story.

Go on a pretend journey.
Use the map you made today to go on a pretend journey. Pack a backpack with the essentials and travel around your house. If you've left your fort up from the day before, let that be your ending place.

Pretend to be stars in the sky.
Stretch your arms and legs out wide. Then, shake and wiggle to shine. Be "shooting stars" and wiggle across the room. End by singing "Twinkle, Twinkle Little Star."

Go outside at night after dark and look at the stars.
This could be as simple as a few minutes outside before bedtime or be turned into a longer event by laying a blanket out on the ground and having some snacks. Try and count the stars together. Talk about how God told Abraham there would be as many people in his family as stars in the sky. If you live in an area that doesn't have a very good view of the night sky, you could also do a Google search for images of a starry sky and look at those while you discuss.

Have a birthday party for Isaac.
This could be done in many different ways. Some ideas are: have a special snack, make decorations, make it a pretend party with play food and dress up clothes, play a party game, etc. Don't forget to sing Happy Birthday to baby Isaac!

CRAFTS

Objective: To learn that Abraham traveled in a tent

Supplies:
- Paper sack (grocery bag or lunch sack)
- Markers or crayons

Prepare Beforehand:
- Cut the top of the paper sack off
- Turn the bottom of the sack upside down and cut out a rectangle for a doorway

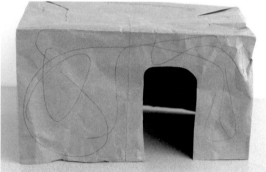

Directions:
Use the markers or crayons to decorate the paper sack to be Abraham's tent.

ABRAHAM'S TENT

Objective: To learn that Abraham went on a long journey

Supplies:
- Brown construction paper
- Markers or crayons

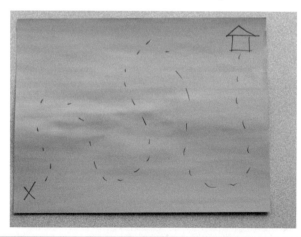

Directions:
Talk about what your child thinks Abraham and Sarah would see on their long journey. Use the brown paper to make a simple map for their trip. Roll the map up and use it for pretend play.

LONG JOURNEY

NIGHT STARS

Objective: To learn about God's promise to Abraham

Supplies:
- Black construction paper
- Yellow or white paint
- Small paintbrush or cotton swab

Directions:
Use the paintbrush or cotton swab to make yellow or white dots on the black paper. Make lots of stars in the night sky!

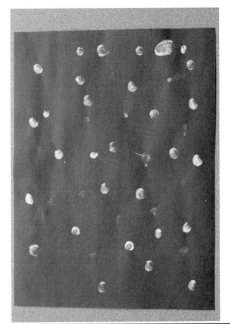

STARRY BANNER

Objective: To learn about God's promise to Abraham

Supplies:
- Yellow construction paper
- Marker or crayon
- Tape

Prepare Beforehand:
- Cut stars out of the yellow construction paper

Directions:
On each star write a member of your family's name. Roll out a length of tape and stick each star in it to make a banner.

BABY ISAAC

Objective: To learn that God kept his promise

Supplies:
- Salt dough* (air dry clay can also be used)
- Markers or paint

Directions:
Form the dough into a long skinny shape for the baby's body and a ball shape for the head. Connect the shapes together. Bake the dough at a low temperature until dry. Once dry, use markers to color the face and body of Isaac.

*Salt Dough Recipe: Mix together 1/2 cup of flour and 1/4 cup of salt. Slowly add water until a dough forms. Knead until smooth.

JOSEPH

Genesis 37, 39-45

Memory Verse

"You intended to harm me, but God intended it for good to accomplish what is now being done, the saving of many lives." Genesis 50:20 (NIV)

Guided Discussion

Parent: Were Joseph's brothers mean or nice?

Child: Mean.

Parent: Yes, they took his coat and sent him away. What did Joseph do in Egypt?

Child: Worked hard.

Parent: When Joseph's brothers came to get some food, was he mean or nice to them?

Child: Nice!

Parent: Yes, Joseph forgave his brothers. Did God have a plan for Joseph?

Child: Yes!

Joseph Forgave His Brothers
- - -
God Had a Plan for Joseph

Teaching Tips

The story of Joseph is a long one, with lots of different sub-stories happening. For children this age range try to keep the story to its essentials, otherwise they will get lost in all the details. A good simple summary of the story is: "Joseph's brothers are mean and send him away. Joseph still loves them." Don't forget to also talk about how "God had a plan for Joseph."

Even though you are keeping the story simple, you can still take time to pause and elaborate on different portions, like Joseph's colorful coat or how Joseph's brothers were very mean. Adding an aspect of pretend play (like wearing a pretend colorful coat or making mean faces) will help your child remember these parts of the story.

Slavery is not something that a toddler is going to have a lot of context for understanding. Focusing on how Joseph had to "work so very hard" is a good way of explaining it on your child's level.

Before you finish the story, have your child guess whether they think Joseph will be kind or mean to his brothers. When you get to the end where Joseph loves and forgives his brothers, do hugs and high fives to celebrate!

SONG

To the tune of
"The Bear Went Over the Mountain"

Joseph went to Egypt
Joseph went to Egypt
Joseph went to Egypt
To carry out God's plan
To carry out God's plan
To carry out God's plan

His brothers sent him Egypt
His brothers sent him Egypt
His brothers sent him Egypt
But God still had a plan

God still had a plan
God still had a plan
Joseph saved his family
Because God had a plan

SNACK

Joseph's Crazy Coat Cookies

Ingredients:
- Person shaped cookies
- Frosting
- Colorful sprinkles or M&M's

Spread the frosting on the cookies. Use the sprinkles or M&M's to decorate a coat onto the cookies. Talk about Joseph's special coat.

SENSORY BIN

Supplies:
- Tall cup
- Peg people
- Oatmeal or other grain
- Measuring cups and/or spoons

Fill the bottom of the bin with oatmeal and place the cup in one of the corners.
Set in the measuring cups and/or spoons. Scatter around the peg people, designating one person to be Joseph. Scoop and pour the grains, using the cup for "grain storage." Pretend to have Joseph collect and pass out the grains.

ACTIVITIES

Play Joseph tag.
Have your child wear something to be Joseph's special coat (such as a robe). Then, pretend to be Joseph's brothers and chase your child until you tag him or her. Once your child is tagged, take the coat and send "Joseph" away to pretend to work. Then, follow asking for food, saying "Oh! You are my brother! Will you forgive me?" Joseph gives a resounding "yes!" and the game ends with hugs and kisses and lots of giggles.

Play "Follow the Leader to Egypt."
Have your child follow behind you to go on the long journey to Egypt. Play follow the leader around the house until you get to the place designated to be "Egypt." Have your child copy you doing different things along the way (skipping, jumping, crawling, singing, etc).

Have a grain collecting race.
Place some balls (or bean bags, or whatever you have available) in the middle of the room (or outside) and have a basket or box in set a ways away. Then, race to collect the "grain" and place in in the basket.

Bake something together.
It can be from scratch or a box - it doesn't matter! Use the time to bring up a discussion about Joseph's grain. Grain is how you get flour and flour is used to make food. Joseph saved his family by making sure they had food to eat.

Do something loving like Joseph.
Talk with your child about how Joseph loved his brothers and gave them grain even though they had been mean to him. Come up with something you can do together to show someone love.

CRAFTS

Objective: To learn that Joseph got a special coat

Supplies:
- Paper grocery sack
- Markers or crayons
- (Optional) Other materials for decorating coat: stickers, paint, paper and glue, etc.

Prepare Beforehand:
- Make the paper bag into a "coat" by cutting up the middle to open it up and cutting out a hole on the bottom for the head. Cut holes on the sides for the arms.

Directions:
Use the crayons, markers, or other materials to decorate the coat however your child would like.

Objective: To learn that Joseph got a special coat

Supplies:
- Variety of colored construction paper
- Contact paper (alternatively: regular paper and a glue stick)

Prepare Beforehand:
- Cut a coat shape out of the contact paper.
- Cut small squares out of the colored paper.

Directions:
Peel the sticky back off the contact paper (you may need to use a little tape to stick it to the table to prevent it from rolling back up). Stick the squares of construction paper onto the coat shape.

Objective: To learn that when Joseph was in Egypt he was put in jail, even though he didn't do anything wrong

Supplies:
- Black construction paper
- White paper
- Crayons or markers
- Glue stick

Prepare Beforehand:
- Cut the black construction paper into narrow strips

Directions:
Draw a person in the middle of your paper (stick figures are perfectly fine!). Glue the black strips around and over "Joseph" to put him in jail.

Objective: To learn that Joseph collected grain

Supplies:
- Brown construction paper
- Oatmeal or other grain
- White paper
- Glue
- Markers and/or crayons (optional)

Prepare Beforehand:
- Cut the brown paper into a large rectangle

Directions:
Glue the brown construction paper rectangle into the center of the white paper and cover with glue. Stick the oatmeal into the glue. Draw a Joseph figure next to your grain.

Objective: To learn that Joseph still loved his brothers

Supplies:
- Red construction paper
- Crayons and/or markers

Prepare Beforehand:
- Cut the construction paper into a heart shape

Directions:
Decorate the heart with the crayons or markers. Just like Joseph loved his brothers and gave them grain, have your child give the heart to someone they love.

MOSES

Exodus 2-14

Memory Verse

"The Lord is my strength and my defense; he has become my salvation. He is my God, and I will praise him, my father's God, and I will exalt him. The Lord is a warrior; the Lord is his name." -Exodus 15:2-3 (NIV)

Moses Led the People
- - -
God Rescued His People

Guided Discussion

Parent: How was Moses saved when he was a baby?

Child: In a basket (in the river).

Parent: Who talked to Moses from a bush and told him to set the people free?

Child: God!

Parent: What did Pharaoh say when Moses said to let the people go?

Child: No!

Parent: Yep, but Pharaoh changed his mind when God sent the plagues. What did Moses and the people go through when they left?

Child: The sea.

Teaching Tips

The burning bush can be a strange concept for a young child to wrap their mind around. A helpful way to explain it can be to say that God talks to people in lots of different ways and this time he talked to Moses through a bush that was on fire!

Another unfamiliar concept that can pop up in the Moses story is the phrase "God's people." At this point, don't feel like you need to delve into this concept in great detail. Simple statements like: "They were the people working hard for Pharaoh," or "They were the people God was going to save," will give plenty of information for now.

Pharaoh can be a fun character for little kids. Explain who he is by saying that he was the mean man in charge of making God's people work hard. Then, talk about how Moses told him: "Let the people go," and Pharaoh said: "No!" Now, you say to your child: "Let the people go!" and he or she can shout back: "No!" What little kid doesn't love shouting the word "no"?

When telling the part of the story where the people leave Egypt, stand up and get out some wiggles by marching in place.

SONG

Sung to the tune of "Hey Diddle Diddle"

Hey Pharaoh, Pharaoh
will you let us go?
We're working too hard for you
Our God is so great, He will save us
And lead us to the promised land too

Hey Pharaoh, Pharaoh
you need to let us go
or plagues will be coming soon
Our God is so great, He will save us
And lead us to the promised land too

Hey Pharaoh, Pharaoh
it's time for us to go
The water we will go through
Our God is so great, He will save us
And lead us to the promised land too

SNACK

Going Through the Sea Snack

Ingredients:
- Blueberries
- Graham cracker

Lay out graham crackers to be the path through the sea. Fill up the plate on either side of the crackers with blueberries to be the parted waters.

SENSORY BIN

Supplies:
- Peg people (at least two)
- Blocks
- Filler (can be green for grass or whatever you have)
- Frog and/or bug figurines

Place the filler material in the bottom of the bin. Use the blocks to build a "throne" for Pharoah to sit on. Place a peg person on the throne to be Pharaoh. Place a peg person in front of him to be Moses. Scatter around the frogs and/or bugs.

ACTIVITIES

Baby Moses water play.
Fill a bin or container with water. Add a baby or person toy and a small plastic container. Float baby Moses in his "basket" and play in the water.

Practice praying.
Say, "we're going to pray to God now!" and show your child how to fold his or her hands. Remembering to keep eyes closed will be tricky for this age, but that's totally okay! Keep the prayer quick - one or two short sentences. Your child may even want to add their own "thank you God for _____" prayers.

Pin the fire on the bush.
Draw a simple bush outline on a piece of paper and hang it on the wall. Give your child a piece of red or orange paper cut into a flame shape with a piece of tape on it. Older kids can try to stick it to the bush while blindfolded, but most children this age will find it fun enough to tape it to the bush without a blindfold.

Play "Pharaoh May I?"
Similar to the classic game "Mother May I?" Have your child be the Pharaoh and you be Moses. Moses says: "Pharaoh, may I take 2 steps?" and Pharaoh says "Yes." Repeat asking different numbers of steps. After doing this a few times, ask: "Pharaoh, may the people go?" and to that Pharaoh says "no!!" and chases you back to the beginning.

Red sea pretend play.
Drape two blue blankets or sheets over chairs, creating a walkway between them. Cut out a few fish from construction paper and tape them onto the blankets. Let your child wear a robe (or even a large t-shirt tied at the waist) to pretend to be Moses. A broom handle, walking stick, or wrapping paper tube makes a perfect staff. Walk through the sea!

CRAFTS

Objective: To learn that Moses was saved as a baby

Supplies:
- Cereal box
- 2-3 sheets of blue tissue paper
- Glue
- Something to be Moses and his basket

Prepare Beforehand:
- Cut out the front and back of the cereal box

Directions:
Fold up the long sides of each cardboard rectangle an inch. Overlap and glue together the two pieces so they become one long run of cardboard. Tear the blue paper into small pieces. Drizzle some glue into the cardboard (with the flaps facing up). Stick the blue paper pieces into the glue to make the water inside your river. After the glue dries, put Moses in his basket and have him pretend to go down the river.

Objective: To learn that God hears our prayers, just like He heard the people's in the story

Supplies:
- Paper
- Crayons or markers

Prepare Beforehand:
- Write on the top of the paper "God can help me"

Directions:
Talk to your child about how God always hears our prayers and wants to help us. Ask your child what they need God's help with. Depending on your child's ability, have them draw or you draw a simple picture depicting their prayer to God. Let them color the paper more if they desire.

Objective: To learn that God spoke to Moses through a burning bush

Supplies:
- Twigs gathered from outside
- Red paint
- Paintbrush
- Styrofoam dome or block

Prepare Beforehand:
- Collect twigs from outside

Directions:
Paint the twigs with the red paint to make them look like they are burning. Stick the twigs in the styrofoam, arranged to look like a bush.

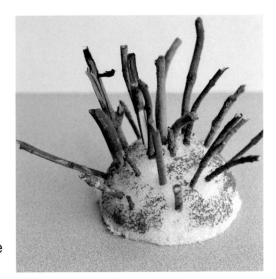

Objective: To be introduced to the concept of the plagues

Supplies:
- Frog and bug stickers (or pictures printed from online and glue)
- Sheet of paper
- Crayons or markers

Prepare Beforehand:
- Draw a stick figure on the sheet of paper (Alternatively, print out a picture of a Pharaoh)

Directions:
Stick the bug and frog stickers all around your paper with the people on it. Talk about how God sent things called plagues to get Pharaoh to change his mind.

Objective: To learn how God kept his people safe through the sea

Supplies:
- Brown construction paper
- Blue construction paper

Prepare Beforehand:
- Cut the blue sheet of paper in half the long way and cut strips along each long side

Directions:
Bend the strips so they are standing up. Glue the blue halves to the brown paper so that the strips are facing in, creating a path between them. Use figurines to walk through the parted sea.

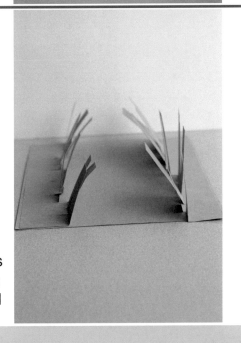

JOSHUA

Numbers 13-14, Joshua 6

Memory Verse

"This is my command--be strong and courageous! Do not be afraid or discouraged. For the LORD your God is with you wherever you go." -Joshua 1:9 (NLT)

Joshua Trusted God - - - God Took Care of His People

Guided Discussion

Parent: When the spies saw the people in the land, how did they feel?

Child: Scared!

Parent: Yes, they didn't want to go there, did they?

Child: No!

Parent: Lots of years later, when they finally did go to the land, what did they come to?

Child: A wall.

Parent: Yep, and what happened when they did what God said?

Child: The wall fell down!

Parent: Yes it did. They could trust God to take care of them.

Teaching Tips

For this story, focus on how God's people were scared to go to the new land that God chose for them. Because they were so scared, they couldn't go to the new land for 40 years! However, when they finally did go to the land, and met the people they were so scared of, God took care of them! They didn't need to be scared because they could trust God. Joshua was one of the only ones who trusted God the whole time!

Some children might find it interesting that the land that they were going to was land that God had promised Abraham He would give them!

When going over the story of the spies, get up and tip-toe around the house like sneaky spies. If you find something scary, don't forget to trust God!

Take lots of time to act out the story of the walls of Jericho. Walk around, play pretend trumpets, and shout really, really loud! Making loud noises is a toddler favorite.

SONG

Sung to the tune of
"London Bridge is Falling Down"

Jericho is falling down,
falling down, falling down
Jericho is falling down, play your trumpet

God will keep His people safe,
people safe, people safe
God will keep His people safe,
we can trust Him

We will go to the promised land,
promised land, promised land
We will go to the promised land,
because God's with us

SNACK

Cracker Sandwich Wall

Ingredients:
- Rectangle or square crackers
- Peanut butter (or other nut)

Spread peanut butter onto crackers (or leave them plain). Arrange crackers on the plate in a pattern like a wall.

SENSORY BIN

Supplies:
- Small blocks (Jenga pieces, alphabet blocks, etc)
- Peg people
- Green filler

Fill the bottom of the bin with green filler to be the grass. Arrange the blocks in the middle of the bin to make a wall. Place the peg people around the outside of the wall. Knock the wall down and then build it up again!

ACTIVITIES

Play "I Spy."
You can play this game the traditional way - "I spy, with my little eye, something red," and then they find the exact thing you were thinking of - OR you can play an easier version. Say: "I spy something red," and then have your child try and find all the red things in the room.

Pray about your fears.
Talk with your child about what his or her fears are. Pray together that God would help them be brave and trust in Him.

Build a wall.
Using your choice of building material (blocks, plastic cups, toilet paper, pillows, etc.), build a wall together. Then, knock it down!

Listen to a trumpet.
Lots of young children won't even know what a trumpet sounds like! Find a recording of a trumpet being played on YouTube and listen to it together. Have a little trumpet dance party!

Knock down the walls!
Use pillows and couch cushions (or something else that's not too hard) to build a wall. Act out the story, walking around, blowing pretend trumpets, and shouting. Then, have fun knocking down your wall.

CRAFTS

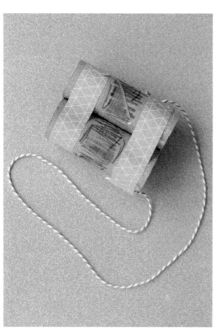

Objective: To learn about the spies who went to look at the promised land

Supplies:
- Two toilet paper tubes
- Tape
- Yarn or string
- Markers, crayons, and/or stickers

Directions:
Use the tape to stick the toilet paper tubes together to make binoculars. Decorate the binoculars with the crayons, markers, and/or stickers. Tape a length of string to the binoculars so they can hang around your child's neck.

Objective: To learn that God's people were scared to go into the new land

Supplies:
- White paper
- Variety of construction paper
- Glue stick

Prepare Beforehand:
- Cut a variety of shapes out of the construction paper that can be used to make faces
- Draw circles on the white paper

Directions:
Talk about how God's people were scared to go into the new land. Ask your child if they can make a scared face in one of the circles using the shapes. Glue the shapes down. Use the other circles to make faces with different emotions.

Objective: To learn that there was a big wall in the way of God's people

Supplies:
- White paper
- Gray construction paper
- Glue stick

Prepare Beforehand:
- Cut the gray paper into small rectangles

Directions:
Glue the gray rectangles onto the white paper in a stone wall pattern.

Objective: To learn that God told them to blow a trumpet

Supplies:
- Paper towel tube
- Markers or crayons
- Plastic soda bottle
- Glue

Prepare Beforehand:
- Cut the top off the bottle

Directions:
Use the markers or crayons to decorate the paper towel tube. Glue the top of the plastic bottle to one end of the tube (white glue will work, but a hot glue gun will dry much faster if you have one available). Play on your pretend trumpet!

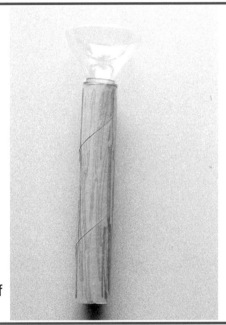

Objective: To learn that the walls fell down

Supplies:
- Two cereal boxes
- Markers or crayons
- Toy figurines

Prepare Beforehand:
- Break down the cereal boxes and cut off the flaps.
- Cut each box in half so you have four pieces.
- Draw a simple brick pattern outline on the pieces.

Directions:
Use the markers or crayons to further decorate the cardboard pieces. Bend the pieces at the folds and set up in a circle to make a wall. Use the figurines to act out the story.

RUTH
Ruth 1-4

Memory Verse

"But Ruth replied, 'Don't urge me to leave you or to turn back from you. Where you go I will go, and where you stay I will stay. Your people will be my people and your God my God.'"
-Ruth 1:16 (NIV)

Guided Discussion

Parent: Where did Ruth go?

Child: Home with Naomi.

Parent: Yes, she was a good friend. How did Ruth work hard?

Child: Gathering grain in the field.

Parent: Yes! And who did she meet there?

Child: Boaz.

Parent: Yes she did. And was Boaz mean or kind to her?

Child: Kind!

Parent: Yes, he let her stay in his field. What did Ruth and Boaz do?

Child: Get married.

Parent: Yep! And they had a baby named Obed.

Ruth was a Good Friend - - - God Took Care of Ruth

Teaching Tips

The story of Ruth is a great one for showing how God is taking care of his people, even when things don't seem to be going their way in the moment. You can remind your child that God is always taking care of him or her, even during the times they have to do things they don't like.

Get moving during this story: walk around the room when Ruth and Naomi are going on their journey home, pretend to gather grain, dance around to celebrate the wedding, and make baby sounds when Obed is born.

Talk about how Ruth was a good friend to Naomi by going home with her and helping her. Ask your child to think of ways that they can be a good friend.

Have your child think of the different ways that God took care of Ruth (giving her grain to eat, Boaz being kind, baby Obed being born, etc.).

SONG

Sung to the tune of "The Farmer in the Dell"

God took care of Ruth
God took care of Ruth
He took care of Naomi too
and he'll take care of you

SNACK

On The Road Snack

Ingredients:
- Apple
- Peanut (or other nut) butter
- Teddy Grahams

Spread the peanut butter down the middle of the plate. Slice the apple into thin slices and lay alongside the peanut butter. Place two Teddy Grahams at one end of the peanut butter "road."

SENSORY BIN

Supplies:
- Girl peg person
- Small basket (or bowl)
- Green construction paper
- Black or brown filler

Place the filler in the bottom of the bin to be the soil. Use real dirt if you want to have some messy play! Cut small strips of green paper and place throughout the bin. Put the basket in one corner and the peg person in the other. Use the basket to "collect the grain" like Ruth.

ACTIVITIES

Traveling home obstacle course.
Use various objects (pillows, blankets, mats, etc) to make a "road" obstacle course. Start in "Moab" and travel through the obstacle course to get to "Bethlehem."

Grain gathering game.
Scatter cotton balls around the room to be the grain in the field. Have your child to race to see how quickly they can put all the cotton balls into a bucket or basket. For added fun, try setting a timer.

Be kind like Boaz.
Together come up with something kind you can do for someone, just like Boaz was kind to Ruth. Once you've decided what to do - whether big or small - do it! The ideas your child come up with may seem silly to you, but it will be very meaningful to them to be able to carry out something that they thought up.

Have a wedding treat.
When someone gets married there are always yummy treats! Prepare a treat together and eat it while talking about the story of Ruth.

Baby pretend play.
Use a baby doll to play pretend about the story. One of you can be Ruth and the other Boaz. Name the baby doll Obed. Let your child lead the play. It's a great way to practice the names of the people in the story!

CRAFTS

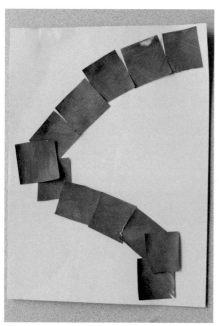

Objective: To learn that Ruth traveled home with Naomi

Supplies:
- Brown paint and paintbrush
- Scissors
- Green construction paper
- White paper
- Glue stick

Directions:
Use the brown paint to cover the white paper. Let dry. Cut the brown painted paper into squares or rectangles. Glue the squares onto the green paper to make the road that Ruth and Naomi traveled on.

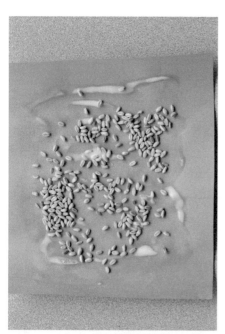

Objective: To learn that Ruth gathered grain in the field to get food for her and Naomi

Supplies:
- Brown construction paper
- Glue
- Grain (oats, rice, barley, etc)

Directions:
Drizzle glue on the brown paper "field" and stick the grain into the glue.

NICE BOAZ

Objective: To learn that Boaz met Ruth and was kind to her

Supplies:
- Green + brown construction paper
- Glue stick
- Magazine with pictures of people
- Markers or crayons

Prepare Beforehand:
- Cut the brown paper into a smaller rectangle

Directions:
Glue the brown rectangle onto the green paper to be the field. Use the markers or crayons to color grain in the field. Cut a picture of a happy man and a happy woman out of the magazine. Glue the man and woman near the field.

RUTH + BOAZ

Objective: To learn that Ruth married Boaz

Supplies:
- White paper
- Markers or crayons
- Red construction paper
- Glue stick

Prepare Beforehand:
- Cut a heart out of the red paper.

Directions:
Draw two stick figures on the white paper - one to be Ruth and one to be Boaz. Glue the red heart above Ruth and Boaz. Color the paper.

A NEW BABY

Objective: To learn that Ruth and Boaz had a baby

Supplies:
- Toilet paper tube
- Markers or crayons
- Piece of cloth
- Glue

Directions:
Use the markers or crayons to draw a baby face on the toilet paper tube. Spread glue on the tube (below the face) and wrap the cloth around it to be a baby blanket.

SAMUEL

1 Samuel 1-3

Memory Verse

"The Lord came and stood there, calling as at the other times, 'Samuel! Samuel!'
Then Samuel said, 'Speak, for your servant is listening.'"
-1 Samuel 3:10 (NIV)

Guided Discussion

Parent: Where did Samuel go when he heard his name called?

Child: To Eli.

Parent: What did Eli say?

Child: It wasn't me – go to bed!

Parent: Who was really calling Samuel?

Child: God!

Parent: Yes, God was calling Samuel to be a leader and messenger.

Samuel Listened to God - - - God Called Samuel

Teaching Tips

Samuel's mom, Hannah, prayed for a son. Talk with your child about the different things that they can pray for, letting them share their ideas.

Act out the scene of Samuel being called, with your child being Samuel and you being Eli. Use a little dramatic flare! It is a funny story for kids when Samuel keeps running to Eli only be told "No, it wasn't me! Go back to bed!"

When learning about how Samuel was called by God to be a leader and a messenger make sure to let your child know that Samuel was just a kid when that happened. Even kids can follow God! What do they think that God wants *them* to do?

God spoke to Samuel when he was trying to sleep. Ask your child if they know the main way God speaks to them. How does God tell us what he wants us to do? The Bible! Look up together a verse in the Bible and read God's Word together.

SONG

To the tune of "Are You Sleeping/Frère Jacques"

Are you sleeping?
Are you sleeping?
Samuel
Samuel
God is calling you
God is calling you
To be a leader
To be a leader

SNACK

Sleeping Samuel Snack

Ingredients:
- Bread
- Your favorite sandwhich filling
- Apple
- Small star cookie cutter

Make the sandwich and cut into a circle shape. Cut pieces of the apple to make a sleeping face on the sandwich. Cut thin slices of the apple and use the star cookie cutter (or a knife) to make stars. Place the stars above the sandwich.

SENSORY BIN

Supplies:
- Two peg people
- Blocks
- Filler
- Black construction paper
- Star stickers
- Tape

Cut the black paper and tape around the inside wall of your bin. Stick stars on the black paper. Put filler in the bottom of the bin and use the blocks to set up two beds. Place the peg people on the beds.

ACTIVITIES

Have prayer time.
Give a reminder of how to pray: fold hands, close eyes, end with amen. As you model prayer, your child will mimic. Quick prayers are best at this age and "thank you God for _____" prayers are easy to remember. Don't forget to remind your child that God always hears our prayers!

Play a "Samuel version" of Red Light, Green Light.
Have your child start on one side of the room, while you are on the other side. When you call "Samuel!" your child can start walking or running towards you. Then, turn around and say "Go back to bed!" and your child has to go back to the beginning. Repeat multiple times, ending with your child getting all the way to you.

Act out the story.
Tuck your child in bed all cozy and snug. Then, go into another room and call out "Samuel, Samuel" and have your child come running. Repeat this process a couple times. Then say: "Samuel, God is speaking to you!" and the next time you call "Samuel, Samuel!" have your child say "speak Lord, I'm listening!"

Have a listening time.
Samuel listened closely to God. Spend some time together, listening to the sounds you can hear. Go outside and close your eyes. Be quiet for as long as your child can stand it and just listen. After listening, talk about all the things you heard.

Play "Samuel Says."
Talk about how Samuel was the leader of God's people. Have your child pretend to be God's people and you pretend to be Samuel. Tell your child to do what Samuel says. Say silly things like "Samuel says: jump up and down," "Samuel says: pat your head," etc. (Don't worry about the "tricking" part of the normal version of this game. Don't give your child commands without saying "Samuel Says." Most kids this age don't get that part of the game, and have fun playing without it.)

CRAFTS

Objective: To learn to pray like Hannah did (for Samuel to be born)

Supplies:
- Recycled container (like a peanut butter jar or a can with no sharp edges)
- Craft sticks
- Markers
- Stickers/washi tape

Directions:
Use the stickers/tape to decorate the jar. On each of the craft sticks, write something to pray for (family, friends, church, etc). Put the sticks in your jar. Pull a stick out and pray for what is on it!

Objective: To learn that God called Samuel

Supplies:
- Brown, black or white, and two other colors of construction paper
- Glue stick
- Crayons and/or markers

Prepare Beforehand:
- Cut three skinny rectangles out of the brown paper.
- Cut a simple person shape out of another color.
- Cut a rectangle out of another color.

Directions:
Glue the brown rectangles onto the black paper in the shape of a bed. Glue the person onto the bed. Glue the rectangle over the person like a blanket. Color any additional details desired.

Objective: To learn that God called Samuel

Supplies:
- •Toilet paper tube
- • Piece of cardboard
- • Lid to a shoebox (or similar)
- • Glue
- • Markers or crayons

Prepare Beforehand:
- • Cut the tube into four equal pieces.

Directions:
Glue the paper towel tube pieces to the bottom of the shoebox lid (white glue will work, but a hot glue gun will dry much quicker). Cut the cardboard to fit in one end of the shoebox lid and glue in place to make a headboard. Use the markers or crayons to decorate the "bed."

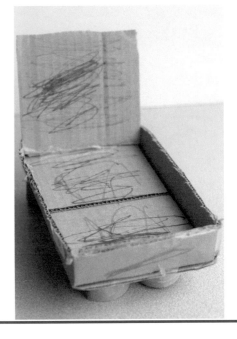

Objective: To learn to listen to God like Samuel

Supplies:
- • Any color construction paper
- • Tape
- • Crayons or markers

Prepare Beforehand:
- • Cut a band out of the construction paper, taping two pieces together if necessary so it is long enough.
- • Trace and cut out two large ear shapes.

Directions:
Use the crayons or markers to decorate the construction paper band. Tape the band together to fit around your child's head. Tape the two ear shapes onto the sides of the band. Talk about using our ears to listen like Samuel.

Objective: To learn that Samuel was God's messenger

Supplies:
- • Brown or tan paper
- • Markers or crayons
- • String or ribbon

Directions:
Crinkle up the paper and then smooth it out to give it a fun texture. Write or color a message on the paper. Roll the paper up and tie with the string or ribbon. Give your message to someone else, like how Samuel gave God's messages to the people.

DAVID

1 Samuel 16-17
2 Samuel 2

Memory Verse

"David said to the Philistine, 'You come against me with sword and spear and javelin, but I come against you in the name of the Lord Almighty'" -1 Samuel 17:45b (NIV)

Guided Discussion

Parent: Who was the big mean guy?

Child: Goliath.

Parent: What did everyone do when they saw him?

Child: Run away!

Parent: But who wasn't afraid of Goliath?

Child: David.

Parent: Yes, David fought Goliath and protected the people. And what did God choose him to become?

Child: The king!

David Was Brave
- - -
God Helped David

Teaching Tips

Little kids usually love making animal noises. So, when you talk about David being a shepherd, give your child a few minutes to pretend to be sheep.

Goliath is a new name that your child will probably not have heard before. When you come to the part of the story where Goliath is introduced, give your child a chance to practice saying his name. Remind them that Goliath was the big, mean, scary guy and let them make their scariest faces.

A good point to contrast is how everyone was scared and ran away from Goliath, but David was brave. Try posing like you are scared and then try posing like you are being brave.

David may seem like the main character in this story, but don't forget that the real main character in all the Bible stories is God. Make sure to emphasize that it was God that helped David be brave and it was God that helped him fight Goliath and protect the people.

SONG

Only a Boy Named David
by Arthur Arnott

Only a boy named David; Only a little sling.
Only a boy named David;
But he could play and sing.

Only a boy name David; Only a rippling brook;
Only a boy named David;
And five little stones he took.

And one little stone went in the sling,
And the sling went round and round.
And one little stone went in the sling,
And the sling went round and round.
And round and round and round and round
And round and round and round.
And one little stone went up in the air...

And the giant came a tumblin' down!

SNACK

Stones and Sling Snack

Ingredients:
- Grapes
- String cheese

Separate the string cheese into smaller segments, arrange on plate to look like a sling. Put one grape into the sling, and set the others to the side on the plate.

SENSORY BIN

Supplies:
- Large figurine/person
- Peg person
- Green construction filler
- Five small stones
- Blue filler

Lay the blue filler across the middle of the bin and the green filler on either side. Place the five stones in the blue filler. Put the large figurine on one side of the stones and the peg person on the other side.

ACTIVITIES

Play "Shepherd Tag."
Have your child pretend to be a sheep and you be the shepherd. Say: "Oh no! My sheep ran away!" and have your child run around the room (or outside). Then, you run around after them, trying to tag your "sheep." When your child is tagged they have to go back to the "sheep pen", which can be a certain corner of the room.

Play "Stone Hunt."
In the middle of the room, lay out something that can be the stones (balls, bean bags, large pom-poms, etc.). Have your child go pick out five "stones" and bring them back to you. Practice counting the "stones" together. To make this more challenging, you could hide the "stones" around the room, making them more difficult to find.

Remember David's bravery.
The next time your child is afraid. Remind them of the story of David and Goliath and how God helped David be brave. Pray together that God would help your child be brave too.

Fight Goliath.
Gather a bunch of soft items that can be used as "stones." If you made the Goliath poster craft, throw your stones at that. If you didn't make the craft, create a "Goliath" by making a stack of pillows against a wall.

Anoint the King.
Tell your child that when David became king, he was anointed with oil. "Anoint" your child by dripping a small amount on water on his or her head. Once you have done this, place a crown on their head and give a cheer for "King David."

CRAFTS

Objective: To learn that David was a shepherd, not a warrior

Supplies:
- Green construction paper
- Black crayon or marker
- Glue
- Cotton balls

Directions:
Spread glue in a large oval shape on the green paper. Stick cotton balls in the glue. Use the black marker/crayon to add a face and legs to the fluffy sheep.

Objective: To learn that David used five stones to fight Goliath

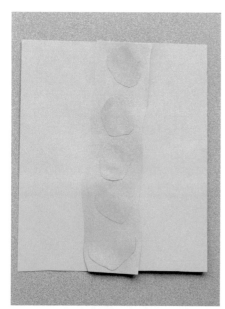

Supplies:
- Green construction paper
- Blue construction paper
- Gray construction paper
- Glue stick

Prepare beforehand:
- Cut out five stones from gray paper
- Cut out a wavy strip from the blue paper

Directions:
Glue the blue strip of paper down the middle of the green paper (this is the river). Glue the five stones onto the blue strip.

Objective: To become more familiar with who Goliath was

Supplies needed:
- Large roll of butcher paper
- Markers or crayons

Prepare beforehand:
- Draw a tall outline of Goliath on a large piece from the roll of paper.

Directions:
Color in the outline of Goliath, adding a face, hair, clothes, etc. After the coloring is finished, hang Goliath up on the wall and have your child stand by him to see how they compare to his size. Use the poster to start conversations about how God helped David be brave.

Objective: To learn that David was brave and fought Goliath

Supplies:
- White and gray paper
- Marker or crayon
- String
- Glue

Prepare Beforehand:
- Cut a stone shape out of the gray paper

Directions:
Trace your child's hand in the corner of the paper. Glue down a string in a loop shape coming from the hand. Glue the paper stone into the string.

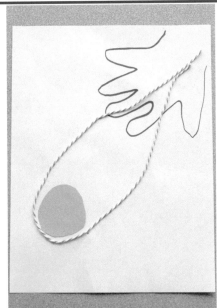

Objective: To learn that God made David king.

Supplies needed:
- Yellow construction paper
- Tape
- Dot markers

Prepare beforehand:
- Cut a crown out of the yellow paper: first, cut the paper in half length-wise, then, cut out one inch segments out of the long sides (like the top of a castle wall)

Decorate the two crown pieces using the dot markers. Tape the two pieces together so they make one long piece. Wrap the paper around your child's head and then tape together.

ELIJAH

1 Kings 17-19;
2 Kings 2:1-13

Memory Verse

Elijah stepped forward and prayed: "Lord, the God of Abraham, Isaac and Israel, let it be known today that you are God in Israel and that I am your servant and have done all these things at your command. Answer me, Lord, answer me, so these people will know that you, Lord, are God, and that you are turning their hearts back again." -1 Kings 18:36-37 (NIV) (Just choose a portion if memorizing.)

Elijah Was God's Messenger - - - God is the One True God

Guided Discussion

Parent: What was Elijah's job?

Child: To give God's messages.

Parent: Who were God's people following?

Child: Fake gods.

Parent: Yes, what did Elijah tell them to do?

Child: Follow the real God!

Parent: Could the fake gods do anything?

Child: No!

Parent: That's right - only God is the One True God.

Teaching Tips

There is a lot going on in Elijah's story. Focus on how God's people, especially the king and queen, were not following Him and instead were following fake gods. Elijah's job was to bring messages from God to remind His people that He is the only true God.

This story is one that can be harder to find in some of the more simpler children's Bibles. Try paraphrasing the story and retelling it for your child or using a children's Bible that has a larger selection of stories (such as The Beginner's Bible).

One thing you could do this week is break up the story by reading a different portion each day.

The story of the fire from heaven is a fun story for kids and a big part of Elijah's story. Ask your child what they think will happen to each of the altars. Who do they think will win the "competition"?

SONG

Sung to the tune of "Three Blind Mice"

One true God
One true God
So powerful
So powerful

They all ran after
the gods that were fake
But God sent some fire
and make the earth shake

Did you ever see
Such a sight in your life
As one true God?

SNACK

Cheese and Pretzel Altar

Ingredients:
- Cheese cut into cubes
- Mini stick pretzels
- Deli meat

Stack the cheese cubes as the base of the altar. Place the pretzels on top. Tear the deli meat into smaller pieces and place on top of the pretzels.

SENSORY BIN

Supplies:
- Small sticks
- Stones
- Blue filler (to be water)
- Peg person
- Toy cow

Set all the materials in the bin in separate piles. Play the story by using the sticks and stones to build an altar for Elijah.

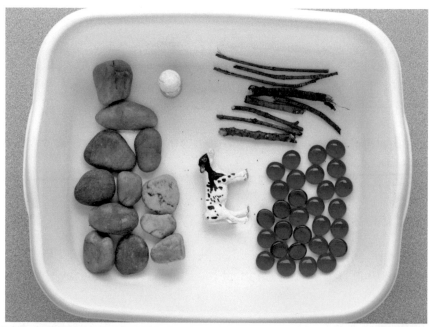

ACTIVITIES

No more rain bathtub play.
Use a cup, shower head, or play watering can to sprinkle water around the bath. When your child says: "God said no more rain!" stop watering. Simple, but fun!

Bird pretend play.
Have a basket with something to be the food (could be play food or just a basket of balls or similar) and an empty basket set up across the room. Pretend to be birds and carry the "food" to the other basket for Elijah.

Make some bread.
Follow a simple recipe to make a loaf of bread. While making it together, talk about how God made the jars of flour and oil never run out.

Altar building outside play.
Gather some sticks and rocks while playing outside. Use them to build pretend altars like the ones from the story. Talk about the One True God while you are playing.

Chariot of fire pretend play.
Use laundry basket or box to be Elijah's "chariot of fire." Push your child around in the basket and talk about how God brought Elijah to heaven in a chariot of fire.

CRAFTS

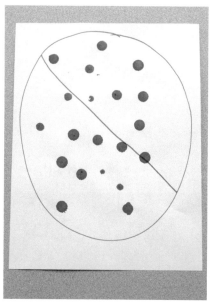

Objective: To learn that Elijah said that it would stop raining

Supplies:
- White construction paper
- Blue dot marker or paint and paintbrush
- Red marker

Directions:
Use the blue dot marker or the paint to make rain drops all over the white paper. After the "rain drops" dry, use the red marker to make the "no" sign over the rain. Fold or roll up your message, if desired.

Objective: To learn that God took care of Elijah by sending ravens with food

Supplies:
- White and black construction paper
- Cracker
- Orange or yellow crayon/marker
- Glue stick
- Googley eye

Prepare beforehand:
- Cut a large half circle and a small circle out of the black paper

Directions:
Glue the black paper down into a bird shape. Add feet and a beak with the crayon/marker. Add googley eye. Glue cracker in the bird's mouth.

Objective: To learn that God filled the jars with flour and oil

Supplies:
- White paper
- Black marker
- Flour
- Cooking oil
- Glue stick

Prepare Beforehand:
- Use the marker to draw a simple jar and jug on the white paper

Directions:
Spread glue on the inside of the jar. Sprinkle the flour onto the glue. Dip your fingers into the oil and spread it around inside the jar.

Objective: To learn that God brought down fire from heaven

Supplies:
- Gray, red, orange, and brown construction paper
- Glue stick
- White paper

Prepare Beforehand:
- Cut the gray paper into 12 small squares
- Cut the brown paper into 4-6 skinny rectangles
- Cut the orange and red construction paper into odd, jagged shapes

Directions:
Glue the 12 squares to the white paper to make the base of the altar. Glue the brown rectangles at the top of the gray squares. Glue the red and orange paper coming down from the top of the paper to make the fire.

Objective: To learn that Elijah went to heaven in a chariot of fire

Supplies:
- Small box
- Red and orange paint
- Paintbrush
- String

Directions:
Use the paint to decorate the box to look like fire. Cut two holes in one side of the box and tie an end to the string in each.

JOSIAH

2 Kings 22-23:1-30; 2 Chronicles 34-35

Josiah Did What Was Right - - - God Spared Josiah

Memory Verse

"[Josiah] did what was right in the eyes of the Lord and followed completely the ways of his father David, not turning aside to the right or to the left." -2 Kings 22:2 (NIV)

Guided Discussion

Parent: How old was Josiah when he became king?

Child: A kid!

Parent: Yes. And did he follow God and do the right things?

Child: Yes!

Parent: Yes, he did. How much did Josiah follow God?

Child: With his whole heart!

Teaching Tips

The story of the boy king Josiah is one that kids can really relate to - he was a kid just like them! Even at such a young age, Josiah chose to follow God. Even though his family chose evil, he chose to do what was right. Just like Josiah, your child can choose to follow God too!

In the context of Josiah's story, the people in Judah (and the kings before and after him) weren't following God and were choosing evil things. Because of this, God was going to send Judah into exile as He had done with Israel. However, because Josiah chose to follow God with all his heart, God waited until after Josiah died to do this. All those details might be a bit above the understanding of a toddler. However, you can mention that Josiah was kind of like Noah - following God even when everyone else wasn't - and that made God happy.

Once again, this is a less common story to find in a children's storybook Bible. Don't be afraid to tell the story in your own words.

If your child hasn't heard the word "temple" before, let him or her know that is it God's house. It is a place to pray and worship God - kind of like a church.

Talk about how Josiah loved and followed God with all his heart, soul, and strength - which is like loving God a whole lot with your whole body! Stretch out real big to show God how much you love Him!

Ask your child how they can follow God like Josiah. What things can they do that are right?

SONG

To the tune of "Itsy Bitsy Spider"

Josiah was the boy king
who chose to do what's right

He always followed God
every day and every night

He found God's Word
was written on a scroll

So he said let's follow God's way
with all our heart and soul

SNACK

Peanut Butter and Jelly Scroll Roll-Up

Ingredients:
- Bread
- Peanut butter
- Jelly
- String cheese

(Feel free to use alternate fillings)

Use a rolling pin or a glass to roll out the slice of bread so that it is thin. Spread on a thin layer of peanut butter and jelly. Roll the bread up. Use a piece of string cheese to tie up the "scroll."

SENSORY BIN

Supplies:
- Blocks
- Peg people
- Green filler (optional)

Stack blocks haphazardly to make a "falling apart temple." Place green filler opposite the blocks. Set the peg person (Josiah) in front of the temple. Pretend to rebuild the temple.

ACTIVITIES

Play King/Queen dress up.
Using dress up clothes, or whatever you have on hand, dress up to look like a king or queen. Talk about what you would do if you were a king/queen.

Play "Fix the Temple."
Build a simple building out of Duplo blocks (or similar) to be the temple. Let your child look it over. Then, have them look away and take a few of the pieces off. Have them look again and take the missing pieces and try to fix the temple like it was before.

God's scroll hide and seek.
Roll up a piece of paper to be the scroll of God's Word. Hide it and have your child search to find it.

Play "Trash the Fake gods."
Have something set up as a "trash can" - it can be a laundry basket or bucket, etc. Scatter around the room something to be the "fake gods" - balls, bean bags, stuffed animals, etc. As fast as you can, run around the room and get rid of the fake gods just like King Josiah and throw them in the "trash."

Love God by loving others.
One of the biggest ways we love and follow God is by loving others. Ask your child if they have an idea of something that you can do to love someone. If at all possible, use their idea!

CRAFTS

Objective: To learn that Josiah was a kid when he became king

Supplies:
- Picture of your child printed on an 8.5x11 paper
- Yellow paper
- Glue stick
- Markers or crayons

Prepare Beforehand:
- Cut a crown shape out of the yellow paper

Directions:
Glue the crown onto the picture of your child, on top of their head. Use the markers or crayons to decorate the crown or add any other desired embellishments.

Objective: To learn that Josiah rebuilt God's temple

Supplies:
- Shoebox
- Two paper towel tubes
- Glue
- Markers or paint and paintbrushes

Prepare Beforehand:
- Cut the paper towel tubes so that they will fit in the shoebox going the short way

Directions:
Set the shoebox on its side and glue in the paper towel tubes - these are the pillars in the temple. Use the markers or paint to decorate. Add further embellishments as desired.

Objective: To learn that Josiah found God's law

Supplies:
- White piece of paper
- Colored piece of paper
- Tape
- Crayon or marker

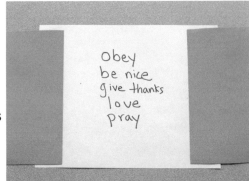

Prepare Beforehand:
- Cut the colored piece of paper into two rectangles

Directions:
Ask your child what some of the things God wants us to do are. Write these things on the middle of the white paper. Lay the two rectangles side by side overtop of where you wrote. Tape the outside edges down. Talk about how God's law was missing, but then Josiah found it (open the flaps!) and wanted everyone to follow it again.

Objective: To learn that Josiah got rid of the fake gods

Supplies:
- Black marker
- Stickers (monsters, animals, silly faces, or something similar)
- Piece of paper

Prepare Beforehand:
- Place stickers on the paper

Directions:
Talk to your child about how (like with the story of Elijah) the people were following fake gods. When Josiah was king, he got rid of all the stuff for the fake gods. Say that you are going to pretend the stickers are the fake god stuff. Have your child use the black marker to color over the stickers to get rid of it!

Objective: To learn that we should follow God with all our hearts

Supplies:
- Red construction paper
- Markers or crayons
- Other craft materials to decorate (if desired)

Prepare Beforehand:
- Cut a large heart out of the red paper
- On the heart write: "Follow God With All Your Heart"

Directions:
Use the crayons and markers (and/or other supplies) to decorate the heart.

DANIEL
Daniel 6

Memory Verse
"Three times a day [Daniel] got down on his knees and prayed, giving thanks to his God, just as he had done before."
-Daniel 6:10b (NIV)

Guided Discussion

Parent: What did Daniel do to get in trouble?

Child: Prayed.

Parent: Who did they tell him to pray to?

Child: The king.

Parent: But who did Daniel pray to?

Child: God!

Parent: So where did they put Daniel?

Child: With the lions!

Parent: Did the lions eat him?

Child: No!

Parent: That's right, God had the angels shut their mouths tight!

Daniel Prayed Only to God
- - -
God Kept Daniel Safe

Teaching Tips

For this story, it is a good idea to spend a little time talking about prayer and how we only are to pray to God.

Daniel obeyed God by praying only to Him. Ask your child how they can obey God.

When you get to the part in the story about Daniel in the lions den, take a moment or two to pretend to be lions.

When you talk about the angel shutting the mouth of the lions, clap your hands together to "shut the lion's mouth."

When the king saw that Daniel was safe, he praised God too! Talk about how when we see the good things God does we can thank him and praise him!

SONG

Sung to the tune of "The Farmer in the Dell"

Daniel prayed to God
Daniel prayed to God
He didn't pray to the king
He only prayed to God

They threw him with the lions
They threw him with the lions
Because he prayed to his God
They threw him with the lions

The angels shut their mouths
The angels shut their mouths
God kept Daniel safe
The lions mouths shut tight

Daniel prayed to God
Daniel prayed to God
He didn't pray to the king
He only prayed to God

SNACK

Lion Quesadilla

Ingredients:
- Shredded cheese
- Tortillas
- Salsa or taco sauce

Cook the quesadilla using your preferred method. Using kitchen shears or a knife, make cuts all around the outside edge of the quesadilla to make the lion's mane. Use the salsa to make the lion's face.

SENSORY BIN

Supplies:
- Brown piece of construction paper
- Peg person
- Lion figurine
- Green and black filler
- Tape

Place the green filler on one side of the bin and the black filler on the other side of the bin. Tape the paper over the top of the black side. Place "Daniel" and the lion in the "den."

ACTIVITIES

Have a prayer time.
Spend some time praying like Daniel. Some ideas of ways you can pray are to take turns praying for people you know, shout out things you are thankful for, or sing a simple song as a prayer to God.

Play "Lion Freeze."
Have your child be a lion and you be the angel. Turn on some music. While the music is playing your child can run around and pretend to be a lion (try using the masks from the craft). Turn the music off and the "angel" shouts "FREEZE!" and your child has to freeze. Turn the music back on and do it again!

Make a den.
Use a blanket or sheet and chairs build a small fort to be a "lion's den." Pretend to be Daniel and the lions.

Play "Saved by the Angel."
Scatter around the room a variety of stuffed animals, pretending they are all lions. Tell your child that he or she is the angel and you are Daniel. You sit in the middle of the stuffed animals, while your child goes around and collects all the animals, placing them in a basket or another designated area.

Have a "praise God" scavenger hunt.
Go on a hunt around your house for things to thank and praise God for. After you find each thing say "Thank you God for this _____!"

CRAFTS

Objective: To learn to pray to God like Daniel

Supplies:
- Any color construction paper
- Glue stick
- Markers or crayons

Directions:
Use a crayon or marker to trace your child's hands on the construction paper. Cut out the hands. Write "I can pray like Daniel" on the hands. Use the crayons or markers to color the hands. Glue the hands together in the praying position.

Objective: To learn that Daniel went in the lion's den

Supplies:
- Paper plate
- Brown, yellow, and orange construction paper
- Glue stick
- Craft stick

Prepare beforehand:
- Cut small strips out of the paper, approximately 2 inches by 1 inch
- Cut the center out of the paper plate

Directions:
Glue the strips of paper around the edge of the paper plate, making a lion's mane. Glue the craft stick on for a handle.

IN THE LION'S DEN

Objective: To learn that Daniel went in the lion's den

Supplies:
- Markers or crayons
- White and brown paper
- Tape

Prepare beforehand:
- Cut a sheet of the brown paper in half lengthwise
- Draw a simple small Daniel and lion on the white paper and cut it out

Directions:
Crumple up the half sheet of brown paper and then smooth it out a bit. Tape the crumpled up piece of paper down to a full sheet of brown paper, making it into a cave shape by taping on either end of the paper. Bend back the bottom inch of your Daniel drawing and tape inside the den.

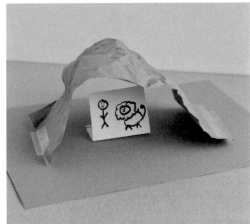

AN ANGEL

Objective: To learn that God kept Daniel safe

Supplies needed:
- Paper plate
- Markers or crayons
- Star stickers (or other stickers, glitter glue, etc.)
- Yellow/white pipe cleaner
- Tape

Prepare beforehand:
- Cut an angel shape out of the paper plate
- Cut the pipe cleaner down and twist into an oval

Directions:
Decorate the paper plate angel however you'd like: draw a face, add stickers, color it in, use glitter, etc. Tape the pipe cleaner oval to the top of the angel's head to make a halo.

THE KING PRAISES

Objective: To learn that after God saved Daniel, the king praised Him

Supplies:
- Yellow construction paper
- White paper
- Glue stick
- Crayons or markers

Prepare Beforehand:
- Cut a crown shape out of the yellow paper
- Draw the king by making a large oval with a face and a simple body with arms (no hands) pointing upward

Use the crayons or markers to decorate the crown. Glue the crown on top of the king's head. Trace your child's hands on the end of the king's arms.

JONAH

Jonah 1-4

Memory Verse

"…I knew that you are a gracious and compassionate God, slow to anger and abounding in love…" -Jonah 4:2 (NIV)

Guided Discussion

Parent: Where did God tell Jonah to go?

Child: Nineveh.

Parent: What did he do?

Child: Ran away!

Parent: And what happened to him?

Child: He got swallowed by a fish!

Parent: Then did he decide to obey God?

Child: Yes.

Jonah Didn't Listen to God --- God Had Mercy

Teaching Tips

Take time to let your child practice saying the new words from this story, like "Jonah" and "Nineveh."

God told Jonah to GO. Ask your child: "what does God tell you to do?"

A good way to help kids relate to Jonah being stuck in the fish is to compare it to a time out. Just like they might have had to go to a time out before because they weren't listening to mom and dad, God made Jonah go in a fish because he wasn't listening to God. Plus, the concept of a "fish timeout" is pretty silly to most kids.

While Jonah not obeying God is a big part of this story and can be especially applicable to kids, don't forget the main takeaway from the story of Jonah is God's great mercy. God's mercy on the city of Nineveh and his mercy on Jonah when he failed to comprehend God's mercy. Don't be afraid to bring this up to your child. They might not totally understand now, but it's still good for them to hear.

While telling the story, let your child get into it with some body motions. Pretend to be on a boat (rock back and forth), jump in the water and be swallowed by a fish (jump and crouch down in ball), and be spit out by the fish (pop up from crouching).

SONG

Sung to the tune of the "Finger Family" song:

Nineveh, Nineveh God loves you
Jonah will tell you what you should do

Nineveh, Nineveh God loves you
Stop doing bad things and love Him too

Children, children God loves you
Trust and obey Him and love Him too

SNACK

"Floating Among the Fish" Snack

Ingredients:
- Fish crackers
- Graham cracker
- Peanut (or other nut) butter
- Teddy Graham

Spread peanut butter on the graham cracker and set in the middle of the plate. Surround the graham cracker with the fish crackers. Place the Teddy Graham on the graham cracker "boat."

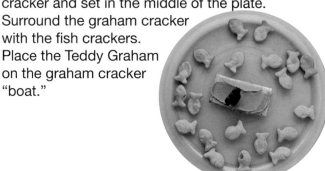

SENSORY BIN

Supplies:
- Plastic bottle
- Permanent marker
- Person figurine (that can get wet)
- Water
- Sea animal figurines
- Blue stones

Cut off the top of the bottle to be the mouth of the fish (if the edges are sharp, run the flame of a lighter over them). Use the permanent marker to add eyes and any other embellishments to the fish. Fill your bin with water, add stones and animals. Put the figurine inside the bottle and place in the water.

ACTIVITIES

"God said GO JONAH" game.
Play like "Red Light, Green Light." Stand on opposite sides of the room as your child. Turn your back to him or her and say "Go Jonah!" and your child starts walking or running. Then, turn and say "stop!" and your child stops. Repeat until your child gets all the way to you.

Jonah on the ship pretend play.
Lay out a blue blanket or sheet to be the water. Place a laundry basket or large box on the blanket to be the ship. Play pretend in the "boat."

Jonah tag.
You are the fish and your child is Jonah. Ask: "When God told Jonah to go to Nineveh, what did he do?" When your child says "run!", tell them to go ahead and run away! Then chase "Jonah" around the room until you catch him. Once you catch Jonah, make him promise to go to Nineveh and then let him go!

Pray like Jonah.
Jonah needed help from God to get out of the fish. But even more importantly, Jonah needed God's help to do the right thing. Ask your child what things they need God's help to do. Spend a few minutes praying together about those things.

Share the love.
God wanted Jonah to go tell the people of Nineveh about God because He loved them. We can share God's love with people too! Together, come up with a way you can show someone love today - and then do it!

CRAFTS

Objective: To learn that God told Jonah to GO to Nineveh

Supplies:
- Paper towel tube
- Markers, including green

Directions:
Use a green marker to color the paper towel tube green (green means go!). Write the word GO on the side of the tube. Use your tube as a megaphone to shout "Go Jonah Go!" and "Go to Nineveh!"

Objective: To learn that Jonah ran away from God

Supplies:
- Brown construction paper
- Blue construction paper
- Blue tissue paper
- Glue stick

Prepare Beforehand:
- Cut a boat shape out of the brown paper
- Cut the tissue paper into small squares

Directions:
Glue the boat to the middle of the blue paper. Glue the blue tissue paper all around the bottom of the boat to be the waves. Draw Jonah on the boat (optional).

IN THE FISH

Objective: To learn that Jonah got swallowed by a fish

Supplies:
- Paper plate
- Paint and paintbrush
- Googly eye
- Marker (optional)
- Glue

Prepare Beforehand:
- Cut a triangle out of the paper plate to make the mouth opening and the piece for the tail

Directions:
Glue the tail on the opposite side as the mouth. Paint the fish and let dry. Add the googly eye. Draw a Jonah stick figure in the center of the fish (optional).

JONAH NEEDS HELP

Objective: To learn that Jonah prayed to God for help from inside the fish

Supplies:
- White paper
- Crayons or markers
- Small tree branch (about 1-1.5 ft)
- Tape

Direcions:
Tape the white paper to the end of the stick to make a flag (mention how a white flag means that you surrender and need help). Write the word "Help" on the flag. Use the crayons or markers to decorate your flag.

JONAH GOES

Objective: To learn that Jonah listened to God and went to Nineveh

Supplies:
- Small envelopes
- Crayons or markers
- Glue stick
- Paper

Directions:
Open the envelopes and glue them to the long edge of the paper to create a row of house shapes. Use the crayons to decorate the houses and draw a Jonah figure walking around "Nineveh."

ESTHER

Esther 1-10

Memory Verse

"For if you keep silent at this time, relief and deliverance will rise for the Jews from another place, but you and your father's house will perish. And who knows whether you have not come to the kingdom for such a time as this?" -Esther 4:14 (ESV)

Guided Discussion

Parent: Who did the king choose as a wife?

Child: Esther.

Parent: Who wanted to kill God's people?

Child: Haman.

Parent: Who saved God's people?

Child: Esther!

Parent: Yes, Esther was very brave and God used her to save His people.

Esther Was Courageous - - - God Used Esther to Save His People

Teaching Tips

There's a lot going on in the story of Esther, so keep it as simple as possible. Details can be added in later as your child gets older, for now just focus on the basics and the main point - that Esther was courageous and God used Esther to save His people.

Get your child involved in the story. During the happy parts (Esther made queen, the people saved) have him or her stand and cheer and clap. During the sad parts (the people being afraid because Haman was going to kill them) have him or her make sad, crying faces.

Before you get to the end of the story, let your child guess if they think Esther will be brave and go to the king.

A good point to talk about is that even though Esther didn't know it, God had a plan for her life (kind of like Joseph!). God had Esther become queen so that she would later be able to save the Jewish people.

SONG

Sing to the tune of "Row, Row, Row Your Boat"

Sad, sad, sad they were
'til Esther came along
Then they turned their frowns around
And sang a little song

SNACK

Veggie Crown

Ingredients:
- Variety of prepared veggies
- Choice of dip

Arrange veggies on the plate in the shape of a crown. Add dollops of dip to "decorate" the crown.

SENSORY BIN

Supplies:
- Filler
- Plastic gems
- Small cups

Place filler in the bin and scatter around the gems. Set in the cups. Search for and sort gems for Queen Esther's crown.

ACTIVITIES

Play "King Says."
Everyone had to do everything the king told them to do. You pretend to be the king, while your child is Esther. Say "The king says _____", giving instructions such as: walk in place, jump, pat your head, etc.

Play "Hide from Haman."
Talk about how in the story Haman was angry and didn't like God's people. He wanted to kill them. Pretend that you are Jews and Haman is going to be coming by - so you need to hide! Find a hiding place together and stay there for a minute "while Haman goes by." Then, play again!

Esther's dinner pretend play.
Set up a pretend feast. Use dolls or stuffed animals to be the people. Turn over a plastic bin to be the table. Use play food (or real if you don't have pretend food) to set the table. Act out the dinner scene of the Esther story.

Play "King May I?"
Play like the game "Mother May I?" Have your child stand on one side of the room, with you on the other. One of you be the kind and one of you be Esther. Ask the "king" silly things, like: "Can I take 3 hops?" or "Can I crawl like a baby?" At any point in the game, the king can say "no!" and then chase the Esther back to the starting area.

Have a party to celebrate Esther saving the people!
Wearing the party hats made during the craft, turn up some music, and dance and celebrate like the Jewish people did when Esther saved them.

CRAFTS

Objective: To learn that Esther was made Queen

Supplies:
- Plain white paper plate
- Crayons or markers

Prepare Beforehand:
- Cut paper plate into crown shapes: 1) Use a pencil to divide the center section of the paper plate into 8 triangles (like cutting a pie). 2) Cut along the pencil lines, leaving the triangles attached at the bottom. 3) Bend up the triangles at the bottom to look like a crown.

Directions:
Use the crayons and markers to decorate the crowns. You can also use other materials to decorate the crowns, such as glitter glue, sequins, paints, etc.

Objective: To learn that Haman was angry (at Esther's cousin) and wanted to kill God's people

Supplies:
- Glue stick
- Construction paper

Prepare Beforehand:
- Cut a large oval out of the construction paper to be Haman's head
- Cut shapes out of the construction paper to make an angry face

Directions:
Glue the shapes onto the oval to make an angry face.

Objective: To learn that God's people were sad and afraid

Supplies:
- Plain paper plate
- Craft stick
- Glue stick
- Markers or crayons

Directions:
Draw a sad face on the paper plate. Glue craft stick to the bottom of the paper plate to make a handle. Decorate with the crayons and markers.

Objective: To learn that Esther had dinner with the king to ask him to save her people

Supplies:
- Magazine with food pictures
- Paper
- Glue stick
- Crayons or markers

Prepare Beforehand:
- Draw a large rectangle on a piece of paper
- Cut pictures of food out of the magazine

Directions:
Glue the food pictures onto the "table."

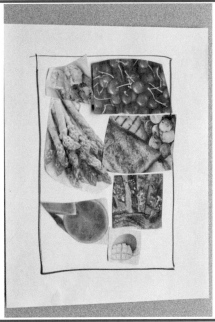

Objective: To learn that the people celebrated

Supplies:
- Construction paper
- Tape
- String
- Crayons and markers

Prepare Beforehand:
- On the paper, draw a large triangle with a curved bottom line (or, google "party hat template" and print one out) and cut out

Directions:
Decorate the triangle with the crayons and markers. Roll the triangle up to form a party hat and secure with tape. Poke holes on either side of the hat and tie a string in each hole.

APPENDIX 1
Recommended Resources

Children's Storybook Bibles:
The Rhyme Bible Storybook (Linda Sattgast)
The Rhyme Bible Storybook For Toddlers (Linda Sattgast)
The Beginner's Bible
The Jesus Storybook Bible (Sally Lloyd-Jones)
The Play-Along Bible (Bob Hartman)

Kid's Bible Based Music:
Seeds Family Worship
Listener Kids
Steve Green's Hide 'Em In Your Heart
The Ology: Ancient Truth's Ever New by Sovereign Grace Music
Cedarmont Kids
Yancy

Ditigal Media:
The Beginners Bible Videos
Saddleback Kids Youtube Channel
The Bible App for Kids (by YouVersion)

Bible Themed Picture Books:
On Noah's Ark (Jan Brett)
God's Wisdom for Little Boys/Girls (Jim & Elizabeth George)
The Boy and the Ocean (Max Lucado)
Psalms of Praise: A Movement Primer (Danielle Hitchen)
First Bible Basics: A Counting Primer (Danielle Hitchen)
Wow! The Good News in Four Words (Dandi Daley Mackall)
This is the Lunch that Jesus Served (Dandi Daley Mackall)
Lost Sheep (Caroline Jayne Church)

Websites:
www.babydevotions.com
www.truthinthetinsel.com
www.christiethomaswriter.com
www.raisinglittledisciples.com
www.faithfullittlehands.com

Don't forget to check out #playthroughthebible on social media!

Adult Bible Reading Plan

Want to read the stories along with your child? Here is a daily breakdown of the passages to help get you started! Toddler got you too busy to sit and read? Try listening to an audio Bible with the YouVersion app on your smart phone!

CREATION
Genesis 1:1-5
Genesis 1:6-10
Genesis 1:11-15
Genesis 1:16-20
Genesis 1:21-25
Gensis 1:26-31

ADAM + EVE
Genesis 2: 1-8
Genesis 2:9-16
Genesis 2:17-25
Genesis 3:1-8
Genesis 3:9-16
Genesis 3:17-24

NOAH
Genesis 6:1-11
Genesis 6:12-22
Genesis 7:1-11
Genesis 7:12-24
Genesis 8:1-11
Genesis 8:12-22

ABRAHAM + SARAH
Genesis 12:1-9
Genesis 13:1-17
Genesis 15:1-9
Genesis 15:10-19
Genesis 18: 1-15
Genesis 21:1-7

JOSEPH
Genesis 37 + 39
Genesis 40-41
Genesis 42
Genesis 43
Genesis 44
Genesis 45

MOSES
Exodus 1-2
Exodus 3-5
Exodus 6-8
Exodus 9-11
Exodus 12-13
Exodus 14-15

JOSHUA
Numbers 13:1-20
Numbers 13:21-33
Numbers 14:1-22
Numbers 14:23-45
Joshua 1:1-18
Joshua 6:1-27

RUTH
Ruth 1:1-11
Ruth 1:12-22
Ruth 2:1-11
Ruth 2:12-23
Ruth 3:1-18
Ruth 4:1-22

SAMUEL
1 Samuel 1
1 Samuel 2
1 Samuel 3
1 Samuel 8
1 Samuel 9
1 Samuel 13

DAVID
1 Samuel 16:1-13
1 Samuel 16:14-23
1 Samuel 17:1-19
1 Samuel 17:20-39
1 Samuel 17:40-58
2 Samuel 2:1-7

ELIJAH
1 Kings 17
1 Kings 18:1-15
1 Kings 18:16-31
1 Kings 18:32-46
1 Kings 19
2 Kings 2:1-18

JOSIAH
2 Kings 22:1-20
2 Kings 23:1-15
2 Kings 23:16-30
2 Chronicles 34:1-16
2 Chronicles 34:17-33
2 Chronicles 35:1-27

DANIEL
Daniel 1
Daniel 2:1-26
Daniel 2:27-49
Daniel 4
Daniel 5
Daniel 6

JONAH
Jonah 1:1-9
Jonah 1:10-17
Jonah 2
Jonah 3
Jonah 4

ESTHER
Esther 1
Esther 2
Esther 3-4
Esther 5-6
Esther 7-8
Esther 9-10

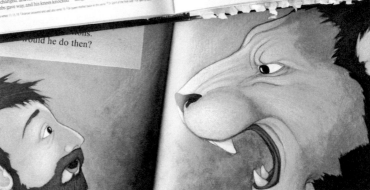

About The Author

Liz Millay ministers to families through her blog, Steadfast Family. She graduated from Cornerstone University in 2009 with a degree in Youth Ministry and Bible. These days, she loves using her education and experience to help parents build strong families and impress God's Word upon their children.

Wife to Dave since 2009 and mom to three precocious little boys, Liz spends her days trying to find time to get the dishes done in-between play-doh sessions and puddle jumping. In her moments of spare time she enjoys being outside, reading, relaxing with her hubby, and spending way too much time on social media.

I love getting to see your sweet little ones playing through the Bible! Please connect with me on social media or use the hashtag #playthroughthebible

@steadfastfamily   pinterest.com/lizmillay   @steadfastfamily

www.steadfastfamily.com

Made in the USA
Columbia, SC
01 July 2025

60163417R00064